SILVERSMITHING AND ART METAL

FOR SCHOOLS • TRADESMEN • CRAFTSMEN

by

MURRAY BOVIN

PUBLISHED BY MURRAY BOVIN

68-36 108th Street   Forest Hills, L.I., N.Y.

Dedicated to my wife, Etta, without whose help this book would not have been possible.

Published by the author of

JEWELRY MAKING

for Schools ● Tradesmen ● Craftsmen

Printed in The United States of America

CONTENTS

BOX CONSTRUCTION

SPOONS, PICTURE FRAMES, SPOUTS

DECORATIVE PROCESSES

SILVERSMITHING AND ART METAL PROJECTS

PREFACE

Before the introduction of the spinning lathe and the development of stamping machines in the early nineteenth century, metal objects that weren't cast were formed by hand.

Today, most metal objects of a decorative and utilitarian nature are formed primarily by machines. Only the very expensive silver object and some copper, brass, etc., objects are made commercially by hand. The handmade tradition currently is carried on mainly in school shops and by hobbyists and designer craftsmen.

It is the purpose of this book to explain with the aid of pictures and diagrams contemporary methods of hand forming silver, copper, and related metals into useful and decorative objects. The information and techniques presented have been gathered, tried, and developed through many years of actual work as a craftsman. All techniques have been tested and the method of presentation has been perfected through years of teaching in high and trade schools, colleges, and adult centers. It is hoped that all craftsmen, students, shop teachers, therapists, and tradesmen can gain useful, practical information about silversmithing and art metal work.

All objects, unless otherwise noted, were made by the author. The same is true of all the photographs and sketches. The author is indebted to many craftsmen who have contributed pictures.

Fig. 1 Basic Tools 1. Domed stake, 2. Chasing tool 3. Raising stake, 4. Round anvil head, 4A Curved anvil head, 5. Divider, 6. Caliper, 7. Jeweler's saw, 8. Tweezer, 9. Hand shears, 10. Engraving tool, 11. Scriber, 12. Needle file, 13. Half-round file, 14. Hand file, 15. Plier, flat nose, 16. Plier, round nose, 17. Plate shear, 18. Raising hammer, 15 ounce, 19. Raising hammer, 7 ounce, 20. Forming hammer, 21. Planishing hammer, 22. Ball peen hammer, and 23. Raising Mallet.

TOOLS AND EQUIPMENT

TOOLS The tools required to do silversmithing and art metal work (fig. 1) are surprisingly few and, with the exception of some of the larger stakes, comparatively inexpensive. The tools listed below are sufficient for starting elementary projects. Specialized tools and equipment will be described as the need for them arises. It is advisable for beginners to write to supply concerns (see appendix) for descriptive catalogues of the tools that are available. It is good economy and safe practice to purchase quality tools.

BASIC TOOLS

These tools are suggested for doing successful craft work. A thorough description of many of the tools will be found in subsequent chapters on processes.

Silversmith forming hammer, 6 ounce
Silversmith forming hammer, 1 pound
Raising hammer, 7 ounce
Raising hammer, 15 ounce
Planishing hammer, 7 ounce
Planishing hammer, 12 ounce
Stake, planishing, round or domed, 2″ or 2½″ diameter
Stake, planishing, 4″ diameter, surface radius—7½″
Stake, "T" type raising stake, 12″ long
Flat anvil head, 3″ diameter
Ball peen hammer, 8 ounce
Mallet, 2¼″ face
Forming block, wood, 3½″ x 3½″ x 5″, with a 2¼″ diameter circular depression (fig. 65)
Shear, hand, 12″, straight blade
Shear, plate, 7″, curved blade
Jeweler's saw frame, 4″ or 6″ depth
Plier, round nose, 5″
Plier, flat nose, 5″
Files, Swiss pattern, 6″ or 8″, 0 and 2 cut, one each, hand (flat) and half-round
Files, needle, 16 centimeter length, one set
Tweezer, 6″, soldering
Tweezer, cross lock type, 6½″
Divider, steel, 6″
Scriber or scratch awl
Ruler, steel, 12″
Engraving tools, flat and round
Caliper, outside, 6″

ADDITIONAL TOOLS It is impossible to list all the required tools since many phases of silversmithing and art metal work such as casting, chasing, and engraving require specialized tools; however, the following should be added as the need arises.

Combination square
Draw plates and tongs
Anvil heads and holder
Aviation shears
Leather covered mallet, 6½″
"Bernard" type pliers
Tongs, crucible, 16″
Surface gauge
Flexible shaft
Blocking hammer

WORK BENCH Almost any sturdy school shop or craft room work bench can be used for forming and planishing metals. The closer the bench is to a window the better, since natural light, especially northern, is desirable. A jeweler's work bench (fig. 2) with a

Fig. 2 Jeweler's Work Bench

tray to catch filings is useful especially when filing and cutting silver and gold.

HAMMERS Silversmithing and art metal hammers can be separated into three classification: forming, raising and planishing.

Forming Hammers (fig. 1-20) Forming hammers, sometimes called embossing, have domed-shaped, round, or oval faces. The hammers are used to form bowls, trays, and plates generally by the "beating down" method described later.

Raising Hammers (fig. 1-18 & 19) Raising hammers have rectangular faces with rounded front and back edges. Several of the smaller raising hammers are sometimes called collet hammers by European craftsmen.

The hammers are used to raise (hammer up) vases, pitchers, and bowls over stakes.

Planishing Hammers (fig. 1-21) The standard planishing hammer has round faces, one of which is almost flat and the other slightly domed. The hammers are used to smooth and to harden the surface of already formed metal objects. The small faceted mark left on the metal's surface by the hammer is a distinguishable feature of a handmade metal object.

Square and rectangular-faced planishing hammers and very wide round ones for trays (fig. 103) are also available.

Converting Hammers Craftsmen can grind and then polish available hammers into silversmith hammers. Thus the face of an eight ounce ball peen hammer can be converted into an excellent planishing hammer.

STAKES The stakes listed under basic tools are essential to beginners. Additional shapes should be added as the need arises.

The planishing surface of a stake must be perfectly smooth and polished otherwise imperfections in the surface of the stake will appear in the metal being planished. Many commercial stakes are made from cast iron; quality stakes are cast or forged from steel. To smooth the surface of a nicked stake, first use a rough file to remove the metal around the nick quickly. Then, with a flat, smooth, single-cut file, draw-file (move the file sidewards back and forth) the stake to obtain a smooth surface. Finally, polish the metal with emery or silicon carbide cloth.

Craftsmen can make their own wood patterns and have the patterns cast in iron or steel at a local foundry. Large cities generally have one or more foundries nearby. Fig. 3 shows two wood patterns and steel stakes cast from them.

TREE STUMPS Tree stumps 26 to 28 inches high and as wide as possible are ideal for holding planishing and raising stakes (fig. 4)

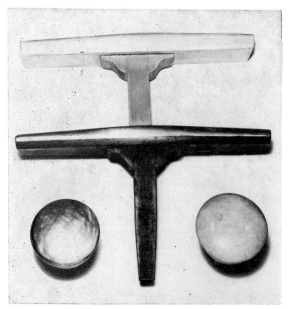

Fig. 3 Wood patterns and cast stakes.

Fig. 4 Stake set in a tree stump

since the stumps absorb much of the hammering noises. Depressions can be gouged into the stumps for forming shallow bowls.

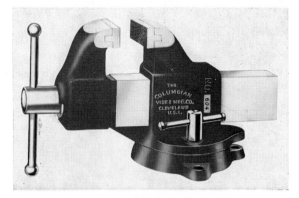

Fig. 5 Bench Vise

VISE A heavy duty bench vise (4″ jaws) is essential for holding stakes (fig. 5). The vise should be mounted on a sturdy bench, preferably over one of the bench legs in order to dull some of the resulting noise from planishing and raising metals.

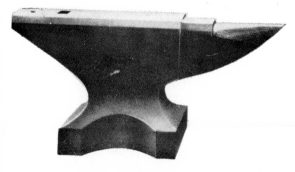

Fig. 6 Anvil

ANVIL A 100 pound anvil is desirable for plate-forming, forging flatware, and many other uses (fig. 6).

SURFACE PLATE A large surface or flat steel plate for truing the bottoms of plates and serving trays is very desirable (fig. 7).

POLISHING (Buffing) MACHINES (fig. 8) Practically any motor can be converted into a polishing machine by attaching a tapered spindle to the shaft. A double shafted 1/3 or

Fig. 7 Surface Plate

1/2 horse power motor with a speed of 3500 r.p.m. is preferred for schools and craftsmen. Professional machines have one or two horse power motors, long spindles, and suction dust collectors to safeguard the health of the workers who use the machines for extended periods.

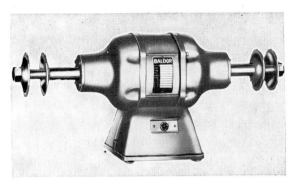

Fig. 8 Polishing (Buffing) Machine

FLEXIBLE SHAFT OUTFIT Contemporary silversmiths, art metal workers, and jewelers find the flexible shaft outfit (fig. 8A) to be an indispensible tool. It is used for drilling, polishing, setting stones, etc. The outfit shown is the bench type. Other outfits are available that can be suspended from the ceiling.

Fig. 8A Flexible Shaft Outfit

SOLDERING EQUIPMENT

The purpose of the soldering equipment is to provide a clean, hot flame quickly and inexpensively for rapid soldering. Since soldering is very important in silversmithing and art metal work, the equipment should be selected carefully. When ordering a blowpipe or torch, specify the type of gas (natural or manufactured) available. Below are several suggestions:

BLOWPIPE A blowpipe (fig. 9) using gas and compressed air is recommended as the least expensive and most desirable method of soldering art metal and silversmith objects. Air can be supplied to the blowpipe by means of foot bellows (fig. 10), an old vacuum cleaner, or an electric rotary blower (fig. 11). A quiet electric rotary blower is recommended. The blowpipes are available in different sizes:—the larger ones are required for soldering medium and large objects.

PREST-O-LITE OUTFIT (fig. 12) Where gas is not available, a prest-o-lite outfit with a pressure regulator is recommended since it is safe and easy to operate, and comparatively inexpensive to use.

The prest-o-lite tank contains acetylene gas dissolved in carbon tetrachloride. The

Fig. 10 Foot Bellows

Fig. 11 Rotary Blower

Fig. 13 Propane Torch

tanks are available in several different sizes. The "B" tank with a number 2 torch tip for small work and a number 5 or 6 tip for larger work is popular in schools. The "B" tank will supply an excellent soldering flame for over 35 hours of continuous use. The acetylene flame is a hot flame, much hotter and superior to the flame produced by propane gas.

PROPANE GAS Soldering torches using propane gas (fig. 13) are comparatively inexpensive initially. They are easy to handle and can be used successfully for small and medium-sized objects.

PLUMBER'S TORCH (fig. 14) A plumber's torch using white, unleaded gasoline can be used for soldering art metal and silversmith objects. Mexican craftsmen (1963) use the plumber's torch exclusively for silver soldering all their silverware: — coffee pots, creamers, service trays, etc.

NOTE: The soldering copper or the alcohol torch is rarely used or recommended for art metal work or silversmithing. The copper can not melt silver solder and with soft sold-

Fig. 9 Blowpipe   Fig. 12 Prest-o-lite Outfit

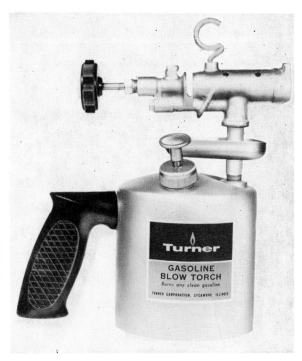

Fig. 14 Plumber's Torch

er the results are unsatisfactory since too much solder can be seen. The alcohol torch is not very satisfactory since the flame is not hot enough for silver soldering large objects, alcohol is expensive, the flame can not be regulated, and too much time is wasted in the preheating process to make the torch work.

SOLDERING AND ANNEALING PAN A soldering and annealing pan (fig. 26) filled with small chunks of pumice is very useful for silver soldering and also for annealing metals since it can be rotated easily so that one can get at all parts of the object being soldered or annealed. The pumice chunks can be shifted to hold objects in position and the pumice, since it will not conduct heat from the metal, shortens the annealing or soldering process.

Note: Be careful when soft soldering on the pan for any soft solder that comes in contact with an object being silver soldered or annealed will pit or burn a hole into the metal.

SUPPLIES Many different items such as pitch, liver of sulphur, and flux are required. All items will be described under processes.

ADDITIONAL INFORMATION This additional information is presented in question and answer form especially for beginners since, it is felt, they may be somewhat taken back by the thorough presentation of the above chapter on silversmithing and art metal equipment.

1. How much money is required by beginners to purchase sufficient tools to get started?

By using some ingenuity and by improvising tools normally available in the average home or school shop, the initial outlay of money can be held to a minimum: to about twenty dollars.

2. What equipment, that is listed, is essential to beginners?

Only the equipment for soldering is absolutely essential to beginners. However, for as little as five dollars a propane gas torch can be purchased and with it small and medium-sized objects can be soldered or annealed. Almost any motor can be converted into a buffing machine, and if a machine is not available several attractive finishes can be given by hand to metal objects. Of course, it is advantageous for craftsmen and schools to have the above equipment.

3. Are there any occupational hazards in silversmithing and art metal work?

With normal precautions, no hazardous conditions that might injure one's health should exist.

4. Can silversmithing and art metal work be done by those living in apartment houses? In private homes?

Apartment Houses:—The noise resulting from forming many average sized objects will make the work objectionable to one's family and neighbors. Many small objects, however, can be made.

Private Homes:—Workshops and even garages are ideal for silversmithing and art metal. Objectionable noises can be reduced by using soundproofing materials that are now available.

THE METALS

WEIGHTS OF METALS Troy weights are used to weigh the precious metals:—silver, gold, and platinum. The base metals:—copper, brass, nickel silver, and pewter are weighed and sold by the standard (avoirdupois) pound. The troy ounce is about 10 per cent heavier than the avoirdupois ounce.

Troy Weight

24 grains .... 1 pennyweight
20 pennyweight .... 1 ounce
12 ounces .... 1 pound

The pennyweight is abbreviated "dwt"; d for the English penny and wt for weight.

THICKNESS OF METALS The thickness of silver, copper and its alloys, aluminum and pewter, is measured by the American Standard or the Brown and Sharpe wire gauge (fig. 15). On one side of the gauge is a group of numbers and on the other side is the thickness of those numbers in thousandths of an inch. The wire or sheet is inserted into the space, not the hole, to find its thickness. **The micrometer** (fig. 15A) is also used to measure the thickness of metals. Most micrometers can quickly measure the thickness of a metal in thousandths of an inch; some can measure to ten thousandths of an inch.

Thickness and weight comparison charts are in the index at the back of the book.

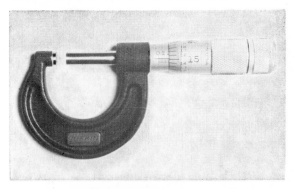

Fig. 15A Micrometer

SILVER

PROPERTIES Pure silver is almost perfectly white, very ductile and malleable. It is the best conductor of electricity. Unfortunately, sulphur and its compounds tarnish it. Pure (fine) silver is too soft for general use; it is hardened by alloying with copper.

STERLING SILVER Sterling silver is an alloy of 925/1000 (92½%) fine silver and 75/-100 (7½%) copper. This proportion is fixed by law. It is the silver alloy that is used commercially and by craftsmen for silverware (holloware), flatware, and jewelry.

COIN SILVER Coin silver, the silver alloy used for U.S. silver coins is 900/1000 (90%) fine silver and 100/1000 (10%) copper.

FOREIGN SILVER Foreign silverware contains varying percentages of silver. In some cases the fineness is as low as 700/1000 (70 per cent). 800/1000 silver is used in France and Italy.

DANISH SILVER Silverware made in Denmark is 830/1000 (83%) fine silver if made to minimum Danish standards. 925/1000 (sterling) fine silver is made for export.

MEXICAN SILVER In former years, Mexican silver sometimes consisted of an alloy with less than a 92½% silver content and the name was given to cheap or imitation silver. Now the sterling standard is used in Mexico and their silver stamped sterling is similar to the sterling silver used in the United States.

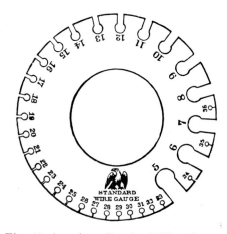

Fig. 15 American Standard Wire Gauge

SHEFFIELD PLATE (originally) was made by bonding sheet silver to copper, rolling to reduce the thickness, and then forming into plate. The original process was abandoned about 1840 due to the introduction of electroplating. Imitations are made by electroplating silver on copper. These are sometimes erroneously advertised as sheffield plate.

SILVER PLATED WARE Silver plated ware is made by electroplating fine silver on to a base metal alloy—usually nickel silver or Britannia metal, sometimes brass or copper. This inexpensive process was perfected for industrial purposes around 1840.

SPRING SILVER Spring silver is sterling silver that has been reduced as much as ten times its original (last annealed) thickness by rolling or drawing to harden it. It is used to make tie and money clips, and where hardness and spring is desired.

ORDERING When ordering silver, the type, thickness, and width or shape must be specified. Sterling silver is the type usually used for silverware. It is sold soft, unless otherwise specified.

Silver may also be purchased half-hard, hard, and spring hard. Half-hard and hard

silver are used for pins and pierced objects that are left flat and do not require silver soldering.

The following chart lists several of the popular sterling silver sheet thicknesses and some of their suggested uses.

Used for	B. & S. Gauge	Thickness in inches	Weight oz. sq. ft.
For flatware	10	.102	.558
	12	.080	.443
For solid handles	14	.064	.351
	16	.051	.278
For holloware	18	.040	.221
	20	.032	.175
For boxes	22	.025	.139
	24	.020	.110
For bezels	26	.016	.087
	28	.013	.071

Sterling silver wire may be purchased in many shapes including round, square, and half-round. Circles of almost any diameter and gauge can also be purchased.

PRICE Sterling silver's price has fluctuated from $1.37½ (an all time high) an ounce in 1919 to 25 cents (a record low) in 1932, to 45 cents in 1936, to $1.00 in 1955, and to $1.29 in 1963. Silver dealers add a service charge to the above price for shaping, cutting, and handling small quantities of silver. **Note:** The value of the silver in a United States silver coin is $1.29 a troy ounce.

TEST FOR SILVER File a deep notch in the piece to be tested and apply a drop of nitric acid.

Sterling silver turns cloudy cream.

Plated ware—the base metal will turn green.

Nickel silver turns green.

Coin silver turns dark or blackish.

Silver when pickled (cleaned in hot sulfuric acid) becomes glittering white; nickel silver takes on a dull gray finish.

Pure silver, when heated to light red and then cooled, remains white; sterling silver turns black (the copper in the alloy oxides).

MELTING POINTS

fine (pure silver) .... 1762° F.
sterling silver .... 1640° F.
coin silver .... 1615° F.

Fig. 16 Rolling Sheet Silver

COPPER

Copper, due to its excellent working properties, its attractive color, and comparative low cost, is one of the most widely used craft metals. Historically, it was used as early as 4500 B.C. by the Babylonians and Egyptians. Today, art metal copper objects, utilitarian and decorative, are very popular in both contemporary and period settings.

PROPERTIES Copper can easily be recognized by its reddish color. Unfortunately, it tarnishes quickly:—often it is lacquered to protect its finish. Commercial copper is practically pure; 99.8% copper and 0.2% arsenic, which is added to harden it. Its melting point is 1981° F. It is a very good conductor of heat and electricity—second to silver.

Copper is very malleable, more so than sterling silver (not pure silver)), brass, bronze, and nickel silver, which means it can be formed or shaped easier than those metals. It can be forged at red heat, but it does not cast well. It is resistant to the action of sea water and the atmosphere. Copper, can not be hardened by heating. When heated until red hot and dipped into water or left to cool in air it becomes soft. To harden, copper must be worked:—that is, planished or hammered, rolled thinner, drawn into a wire, etc. Unfortunately too, silver soldering, will leave the copper soft. Most copper art metal objects must be planished after being silver soldered (not soft soldered) so that they will be sufficiently hard to retain their shape.

ORDERING When ordering copper, state the thickness, hardness, and size or shape desired. Copper and its alloys can be purchased soft, half-hard and hard.

Soft copper is classified into two groups: namely, hot rolled and cold rolled annealed. Hot rolled means, as the name implies, that the copper was rolled into sheets while it was hot and thus the final product (due to the heat) is soft. A harder and smoother copper is obtained by rolling the copper into sheets while it is cold. The copper is then annealed (see page 28) if a soft smooth sheet is desired.

Cold rolled annealed copper should be ordered for most art metal objects since it is smoother and more malleable than hot rolled copper which is usually pitted with small imperfections.

It is advisable to order half-hard or hard copper for making such items as book ends, letter openers, and other objects which do not require much forming and which should be hard when completed in order to retain their shape.

Soft (annealed) copper is obtainable in rolls and in sheets. The rolls usually run from 8″ to 18″ wide and from 18 gauge to 36 gauge in thickness. The standard sheet size is 36″ by 96″ and the gauges run from 8 to 26.

Half-hard copper is obtainable in strip and sheets from 6″ to 48″ wide and in lengths usually up to 96 inches.

The following chart lists several of the popular copper sheet thicknesses and some of their suggested uses in art metal work.

Used for	B. & S. Gauge	Thickness in inches	Weight oz. sq. ft.
Bookends, handles	14	.0648	48
	16	.0486	36
	17	.0432	32
Large plates, bowls	18	.040	30
Smaller objects	20	.0324	24
	22	.0243	18
	24	.020	15
Tooling plaques	32	.0081	6
	35	.0054	4

Most craftsmen purchase 18 and 20 gauge copper. Copper is also obtainable in the form of wire, tubing, rods, circles, etc.

PRICE The price of copper has fluctuated from 18 cents a pound in 1933 to 95 cents in 1963. The above prices are the cost per pound when ordering fifty pounds of the same gauge of copper. Copper dealers add a service charge to the above price for cutting, shaping, and handling small quantities of the metal.

BRASS

Brass is an alloy of copper and zinc;—the zinc proportion varies from 5% to 40%. The proportion is changed for different uses, and occasionally small amounts of tin and lead are added for special purposes.

The brasses may be divided into two groups; namely, the Low-Zinc Brasses with a zinc content of less than 30%, and the High-Zinc Brasses with a zinc content of 30% to 40%.

The color of brass varies widely with the composition:—from the bronze and golden colors of The Low-Zinc Brasses to the yellow of the High-Zinc Brasses. **Note:** 5% zinc and 10% zinc-copper alloys because of their color are known as "commercial bronze" in supply houses, even though they are true brasses. The low-zinc brasses are more ductile and corrosion resistant than the high-zinc brasses and also have superior cold working properties. The high-brasses are stronger, harder, and wear better. Forging brass, 60% copper, 38% zinc, and 2% lead has remarkable heat working properties but cannot be worked cold to any great extent.

Below are the composition and uses of four brasses important to art metal workers.

Gilding:
95% copper, 5% zinc, has a deep bronze color, used for costume jewelry, medals.

Red Brass:
85% copper, 15% zinc, looks like gold, used for costume jewelry, builders' hardware.

Yellow brass:
65% copper, 35 % zinc, has a bright yellow color, most widely used of all brasses.

Commercial bronze:
90% copper, 10% zinc, has a typical bronze color. Used for store fronts, screens, costume jewelry.

Brass is less malleable than copper but is harder, stronger, and can be filed and machined easier. Most brasses cannot be forged at red heat—they crack—can be cast and welded, and do not tarnish as easily as copper. Brass is the base metal for much of the gold plated costume jewelry. Yellow brass, especially when highly polished, has a beauty of its own and is very popular for art metal objects such as lamps, vases, trays, boxes.

Melting Points

Gilding	1949° F.
Red Brass	1877° F.
Yellow brass	1706° F.

BRONZE

Formerly, bronze was considered an alloy of copper and tin. The following two alloys were popular:

Coinage: 95% copper, 5% tin; for coins and statues

Bell Metal: 80% copper, 20% tin; for making bells

Today, modern bronzes contain, besides copper and tin, other elements such as phosphorus and aluminum, forming alloys which are rarely used by craftsmen. Several modern copper alloys are called bronzes, because they look like bronze, even though they do not contain tin. Example:—commercial bronze: 90% copper, 10% zinc. This alloy can be worked cold and is recommended when a bronze-appearing object is desired.

Note:—bronze is tougher and harder to shape by hand processes than copper.

NICKEL SILVER

Nickel silver, sometimes called German silver, is an alloy of copper, zinc, and nickel. Since it does not corrode readily, it is used for inexpensive tableware and imitation silver articles. This alloy — 65% copper, 17% zinc, 18% nickel—is a popular base metal for silver plated flat and holloware. The above alloy has a melting point of 2030° F.

PEWTER

Pewter in Colonial America and in eighteenth century Europe, before the introduction of inexpensive earthenware and china, was used to make household utensils such as plates, spoons, beakers, and salt cellars.

Pewter then was an alloy of approximately 80% tin and 20% lead and since the alloy has a low melting point it was easy to cast in molds. Unfortunately, due to its lead content, the surface of the metal would eventually become grayish-black.

Modern pewter is a Britannia metal alloy of approximately 90% tin, 9% antimony and 1% copper. Its color is slightly duller than silver's and it does not tarnish readily. Pewter is very malleable and does not require annealing. Pewter can be soldered easily; however, since its melting point (app. 475° F.) is not much higher than 62-38 soft solder (356° F.), care must be taken not to overheat and thus melt it when soldering with 62-38 solder. A low melting (200° F.) bismuth solder is recommended for soldering pewter. Pewter is soft and bends fairly easily and for that reason thicker gauges than those used for similar sized copper objects should be used.

Pewter's price, due to its high tin content, is comparatively high—approximately $1.60 a pound in 1963.

ALUMINUM

Aluminum, the most abundant of all the metallic elements found in the earth's crust, was first isolated chemically in 1825 and produced commercially in 1886. It is a light metal: — approximately 1/3 the weight of copper and 1/4 the weight of silver.

Aluminum is a good conductor of electricity. It can be cast, forged, and welded; however, of special interest to craftsmen, it can not be soldered easily at present. It is not attacked by sulfuric or nitric acid—hydrochloric acid and strong alkalis will dissolve it. Many alloys of aluminum are used in industry. For craft purposes "2S" aluminum — commercially pure with slight impurities of iron and silicon—is used.

The color of aluminum is a little duller than silver's. It is popular when planished and given either a high polish or a steel wool or wire brush satin finish.

Melting point is 1220° F.

BRITANNIA METAL

Britannia metal, also known as white metal by jewelers, is the modern industrial name for pewter. It is used, since it can be spun and cast easily, as a base metal for inexpensive silver plated holloware.

Fig. 17 Pewter Teapot   **Fred Fenster**

METAL WORKING TECHNIQUES

1. SOLDERING

Soldering is a method of uniting metals by means of a more fusible, lower melting, metal alloy. It is generally classified into two divisions: hard and soft. The hard solders are the strong, high melting, silver, gold, and platinum solders; the soft are the comparatively weak, low melting, tin-lead alloy solders. In both cases three things must be considered: the flux or substance employed to keep the solder and metal clean, the solder used, and the amount of heat to be applied to the metal.

The purpose of the flux: Most metals oxidize when heated. The oxide prevents the solder from adhering and flowing. The flux facilitates the adherance and flow of the solder by:

1. Forming a protective film to keep the air away from the metal thus checking oxidation.

2. Dissolving small amounts of oxide that have formed.

HARD SOLDER FLUXES

BORAX Borax has been used as a flux for many years and is still preferred by most silversmiths and art metal workers. Powdered house-hold borax (purchased in grocery stores) can be used and when used it is mixed with water to form a thin paste. It is then applied with a brush to the metal to be soldered.

BORAX AND BORIC ACID A 75% borax and 25% boric acid combination is used by several of the large commercial silverware manufacturing concerns as a flux for medium and high melting silver solders. At higher temperatures (see chart below) this combination is superior to borax in checking oxidation of the metals being soldered. The combination is mixed with water to form a paste and is then applied with a brush to the entire joint and surrounding metal being soldered.

COMMERCIAL PREPARATIONS In recent years, several commercially prepared fluxes have appeared on the market in both paste and liquid form. Handy and Harman's paste flux is excellent when used with low melting (1325° F.) silver solders since it is fluid at lower temperatures than borax.

AMMONIUM PHOSPHATE DIBASIC 1 oz. of ammonium phosphate dibasic added to a quart of a saturated solution of 75% borax and 25% boric acid gives the composition of the commercial green tinted liquid flux sold by many supply houses. The saturated solution is formed by dissolving excessive quantities of the above combination in boiling water. **Note:**—the ammonium phosphate is added to a cool saturated borax and boric acid solution to avoid a strong ammonia odor which would be obtained if added to a hot solution. The green color is obtained by means of a dye:—sodium fluorescein.

THE HARD SOLDERS

SILVER SOLDER Silver solder, an alloy of silver, copper, and zinc, is the solder used for silverware and copper, brass, bronze, and nickel silver objects when very strong joints (tensile strength of silver solder—50,000 lbs.) are required. The melting point of the solder depends upon the percentage of zinc: as the percentage of zinc increases, the melting point of the solder decreases. Too much zinc however, is detrimental to the metals being soldered, because zinc burns holes into the metals at high temperatures and the zinc also turns blackish. Metalworkers usually buy silver solders in three different grades: easy, medium, and hard flow. The chart below lists the chemical composition, melting point, and flow point of the silver solders.

Solder	Silver	Copper	Zinc	Melting Point	Flow Point
Easy	65%	20%	15%	1280° F	1325° F
Medium	70%	20%	10%	1335° F	1390° F
Hard	75%	22%	3%	1365° F	1450° F

Note that the solders do not flow at the melting point but at a higher temperature—the flow point. On objects which require several soldered pieces, use a hard flow solder first and then an easier flow. A very low melting (1175° F.) silver solder is available for soldering joints and catches to jewelry

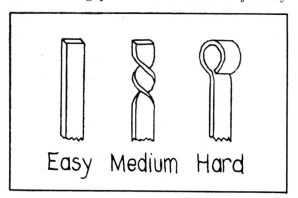

Fig. 18 Method of distinguishing strip solders

objects. For objects to be enameled, a high flowing solder (1460° F) is used.

Silver solders for silverware and art metal objects can be purchased in strip, wire, or sheet form. Strip solder is popular with most silversmiths. 1/32″ by 1/16″ strip is recommended for light objects and 1/16″ by ⅛″ strip is recommended for heavier soldering operations. The strip is purchased in lengths of 1 foot and longer.

This method of distinguishing the three different melting point strip solders from

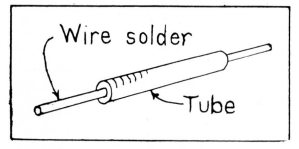

Fig. 18A Wire solder held in a tube

one another can be used. Leave the easy flow solder plain; twist (fig. 18) one end of the medium flow strip solder; form a loop on one end of the high flow solder.

12 and 14 gauge wire silver solder is also popular, especially with commercial silver jewelers. Wire solders are often held in a

narrow tube (fig. 18A) with an inside diameter the same gauge as the wire. This way it is easy to hold small pieces of wire and on production work, since silver is a very good conductor of heat, the solder can be held without burning one's hand.

Sheet solders are used mainly by jewelers. 26 and 28 are practical thicknesses. Sheet solder is cut into approximately 1/16″ to ⅛″ squares by first cutting strips of the required width straight up the solder almost to the top. Then cut across the solder to form as many squares as the job requires. (fig. 19).

HARD SOLDERING PROCEDURE

Hard soldering can best be described by dividing the procedure into four divisions, namely, cut solder, strip solder, poker soldering, and sweat soldering.

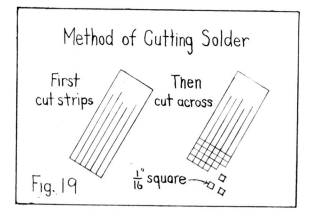

CUT SOLDER The cut solder method of hard soldering is the easiest for beginners to master and for that reason it is described first. The method is especially suited for jewelry and also small silver and art metal objects or parts.

A round narrow base (see base of bowl fig. 64) will be used to describe the method. The band is formed from a strip of metal, bent over a "T" stake, the edges are filed to form a perfect seam, and finally the band is held together as shown in figure 20. Place the band between asbestos blocks (fig. 20) or over lump pumice. Apply flux to the seam. Warm the metal until the water in the flux evaporates and then apply more flux for the flux adheres better to the warm metal. Apply one or two pieces of solder to the seam.

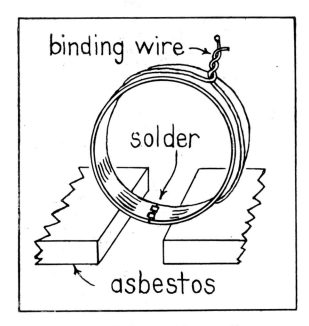

Fig. 20 Soldering with cut solder

A cylinder made from sheet metal will be used to describe the method. The edges of the cylinder must be filed so that they meet to form a perfect seam. Binding wire may be used to hold the cylinder together.

Apply flux to both the inner and outer surfaces of the seam. Place the cylinder, as shown in figure 21, on asbestos sheet, lump pumice, or between two bricks.

Heat the metal and then apply more flux to the seam for the flux adheres better when the metal is hot. Now heat the metal until it is hot enough for the solder, first by heating the metal furthest away from the seam (that is by preheating the metal) and then by heating around the seam directly. Finally, direct the flame at the outer edge of the cylinder until the metal around the seam turns bright red. Make sure that both sides of the seam are equally red and if necessary move the torch from one side to the other so that both sides of the seam become equally red at the same time.

When the metal around the seam is bright red, and while still applying the heat, touch the strip solder to the outer edge of the seam. The solder will melt and flow along the seam. As soon as the solder melts and flows, remove the strip solder from the metal in order to avoid applying too much solder.

Now heat the metal directly, first by heating the band furthest away from the seam (that is by preheating) and then by heating both sides of the seam evenly until the metal turns red and the solder melts and flows. Often the solder forms a small ball before it melts. Remove the heat immediately after the solder flows in order to avoid melting the band too. After the band has cooled sufficiently, remove the binding wire and pickle the band to clean it.

Note:—If one side of the band is heated more than the other, the solder will run up the hotter side. To bring the solder down to the seam or to push the solder back into position if it jumps out of position before it melts, use a poker. A poker is made as described under poker soldering.

STRIP SOLDER With strip solder, silver and art metal objects can be hard soldered cleanly and at a much faster rate than is possible with the cut solder method. The method calls for perfect timing and coordination between the heating of the metal and the application (touching) of the strip solder to the metal. However, with a little practice, one should be able to develop the necessary ability to solder well with strip solder. The saving in time will warrant the practice.

Fig. 21 Silver soldering with strip solder

Move the flame along the seam towards the other side of the cylinder. The solder should flow along with the heat. If necessary, apply more solder and then continue to move the torch until the solder flows to the other side of the cylinder. Long cylindrical objects can be turned and solder can be applied to the other outer edge.

Note: It is best to apply (touch) strip solder to the seam from below the torch's flame, for if the strip solder is applied from above the flame level, since heat rises, the heat from the flame is apt to melt the solder before it even reaches the metal. In other words, the metal itself must be sufficiently hot to melt the solder, and by applying the strip solder from below the torch's flame it can be melted by the metal's heat only.

POKER SOLDERING Pokers are made from 1/16" to ⅛" diameter steel. 6" lengths are used for jewelry and also small silverware and art metal objects. 18" and longer lengths are popular with silversmiths and art metal workers for large objects. One end of the poker is filed or ground to a long, slender point; the other end is bent to form a hook eye so that it can be hung when not in use.

Quick, accurate, clean soldering can be done with a poker as follows: Place a small piece of solder on an asbestos or charcoal block and then heat the solder until it melts and forms a ball (fig. 22-A). While heating the solder, touch the tip of the poker to it (fig. 22-B). The solder will adhere to the poker. Now heat the metal to be soldered to the proper temperature (cherry red) and while heating, touch the solder, still on the tip of the poker, to the seam (fig. 22-C). The solder will melt and flow into the seam. Immediately after the solder flows, remove the poker and the heat.

The poker can be used to apply solder, while the metal being soldered is still hot, to spots that would be difficult to get to with strip solder. It can also be used to shift parts, while they are hot, that have moved out of position.

SWEAT SOLDERING A flat piece can best be soldered to a larger main part by first melting pieces of solder onto the back of the flat piece (fig. 23). When cool, place the flat piece where desired on the main part, clamp or bind in position if necessary, and then heat both metals until the solder remelts. Remember:—preheat the large main part first and then bring the heat gradually to the flat piece.

HARD SOLDERING HINTS

A flux must be used with all metals. Apply the flux to both the metal and the solder. It

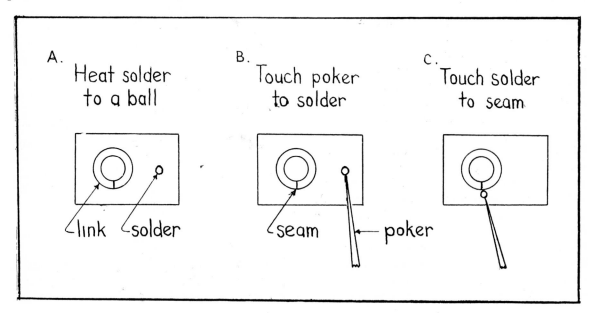

Fig. 22 Method of soldering with a poker

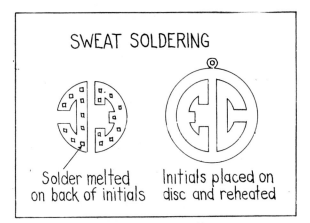

SWEAT SOLDERING

Solder melted on back of initials

Initials placed on disc and reheated

Fig. 23 Sweat soldering procedure

is best after applying a coating of flux to warm the metals slightly and then to apply more flux. Flux adheres better to the warm metal.

Cleanliness is essential. Oxides, dirt, and grease must be removed by pickling, filing, emerying, or scraping. However, it is not necessary to pickle the object after each soldering for the flux will keep the metal clean. If the object looks clean, do not pickle until all the soldering operations are done.

The seam must fit perfectly. Do not attempt to fill in holes with solder for in subsequent soldering the solder will run out leaving objectionable spaces.

Solder with a soft blue flame. Too much air will produce a sharp flame that tends to oxidize and burn the solders and metals quickly.

For cut solder:—heat the metals, not only the solder, for the metals must be hot enough to melt the solder. You can not melt solder onto a cold metal. In other words, heat the area around the seam first (preheat) and then heat the seam and solder directly.

For strip solder:—heat the area around the seam first and then heat the seam directly until red hot before applying the solder.

Solder will run to the hottest metal or part of a metal. When soldering a smaller part to a larger, apply the heat to the larger first for if the smaller part is heated first, it will become red quickly and the solder will flow to it. The torch must be directed on both metals so that they become equally hot at the same time. Occasionally, while soldering, lift the torch and thus the flame from the metal for a fraction of a second to permit the heat to travel evenly to both metals being soldered.

Balling or bunching of the solder is usually due to under-heating or improper fluxing.

The brown glaze material on the seam after soldering is the flux; it is removed by pickling.

Do not attempt to hard solder an object that has soft solder on it. Soft solder when heated to red heat will burn into the metal.

When soldering, the temperature of the metal can be judged by its color. Below are approximate temperatures.

First red	900° F.
Dull red	1100° F.
Cherry red	1400° F.
Salmon red	1660° F.
14K yellow gold melts ..	1615° F.
Sterling silver melts	1640° F.
Copper melts	1981° F.
White heat	2100° F.

Most silver solders flow at about cherry heat or lower. Care must be taken not to heat silver much above cherry heat when soldering or it will melt.

Large objects, silver, copper, etc., are best silver soldered on lump pumice, held in a rotating annealing or soldering pan.

Small silver, copper, and gold jewelry objects are soldered on a charcoal or asbestos block.

Irregularly shaped small metal objects can be soldered in powdered asbestos. The powdered asbestos is mixed with water and molded to the desired shape so that the parts to be soldered lay properly. Sometimes the asbestos is formed into a thick, flat piece and a hollow is carved into it of the desired shape. Carborundum grains (# 12 or 16) can also be used for soldering irregularly shaped objects.

SOFT SOLDERS

Soft solders are alloys of tin and lead. Though they are comparatively easy to handle and have low melting points (approx. 400° F), they do not possess great strength and their white color is very noticeable. They are not suitable, nor should they be used for sterling silverware. Nor should they be used on objects that are to be hammer formed (raised) for, since they are weak, the soldered seam will part.

Soft solders, however, are ideal for soldering parts such as rims, handles, legs, and other attachments to copper and brass objects, and also to silver plated (before being plated) ware. Since soft solders have comparatively low melting points, the heat required to melt them isn't sufficient, as it is with silver solders, to anneal (soften) the metals being soldered. Thus the soldered object is hard and doesn't require planishing (hammer hardening), as do many silver soldered objects.

SOFT SOLDER FLUXES

GLYCERINE AND MURIATIC ACID Glycerine and muriatic acid is an excellent flux for copper and its alloys, and also pewter. It is used by many of the commercial silver plated ware manufacturers. **Formula:** — to one ounce of glycerine add five drops of muriatic acid. Apply to the metal with a brush.

ZINC AND MURIATIC ACID. Zinc and muriatic acid is a popular flux with sheet metal workers. It is prepared by dropping small pieces of zinc into muriatic acid until all chemical action ceases and the solution turns white.

COMMERCIAL PREPARATIONS There are several good commercial preparations that can be purchased in the form of a paste, salt, or liquid. "No-Ko-Rode" is the paste form that is recommended.

THE SOFT SOLDERS

Tin and lead may be mixed in any proportion to produce a soft solder. The most popular soft solder for art metal work is 60-40, which is 60 per cent tin and 40 per cent lead. 62 per cent tin and 38 per cent lead is the soft solder with the lowest possible melting point. Note from the melting points below that soft solder has a lower melting point than its components.

Melting Points

Tin	450° F.
Lead	620° F.
50-50 solder	442° F.
60-40 solder	395° F.
62-38 solder	356° F.

Soft solder can be purchased as a wire, a bar, as a hollow wire with a flux in the hollow, or cut into small pieces. Wire solder is recommended for art metal work.

BISMUTH SOLDER Bismuth solder is an alloy of bismuth, tin, and lead. Its melting point (200° F. appr.) is lower than that of soft solder; therefore, it is preferred by some craftsmen for soldering pewter.

SOFT SOLDERING PROCEDURE

Soft solder can best be described by dividing the procedure into two divisions, namely, cut solder and wire solder.

CUT SOLDER The cut solder method of soft soldering is the easiest for beginners to master and for that reason it is described first. Cut solder is obtained by cutting wire solder into small pieces. If the wire solder is thick it is best to roll or hammer the solder to reduce its thickness and then to cut it to the desired size.

A base soldered to a copper bowl will be used to describe the soldering method. The base is filed to match the shape of the bowl where it is to be placed and soldered. The

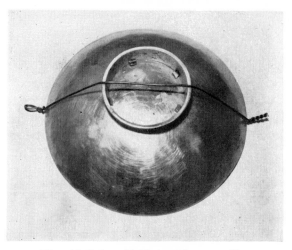

Fig. 24 Soft soldering with cut solder

24

Fig. 25 Scraper for removing excess solder

base piece is then held to the bowl with binding wire as shown in figure 24 or it may rest on the bowl, if it fits properly, without binding wire. Apply soft soldering flux to the seam and then place several small pieces of cut soft solder evenly spaced around the seam as shown in the picture.

Now preheat the metal, first away from the base and then slowly bring the heat up to the base. Use a large soft flame and apply only enough heat to the metal to make the solder flow. As soon as the soft solder melts and flows remove the heat for if the metals are overheated, the flux will evaporate, the metals then will oxidize quickly and turn black, and the solder will not flow. After the solder has flowed around the seam, let the metal cool for a moment until the solder hardens, then the object may be placed in water to cool quickly. Undesirable solder on the inside of the base can be removed with a scraper (fig. 25); solder on the outside of the base can be removed with a file.

WIRE SOLDER With wire solder, copper and other art metal objects can be soft soldered cleanly and at a much faster rate than is possible with cut soft solder.

The same type of example (a base soldered to a copper bowl) as used for describing the soft solder method will be used to describe this method. The base is filed, fitted, and bound to the copper bowl (fig. 26). Flux is applied and then the metals are heated with a soft flame. Care must be taken not to overheat the metals for if they are they will oxidize and the solder, when applied, will not flow. The proper temperature for applying the wire solder is reached when the flux begins to turn to a light brown color. Remove the heat then and touch the wire solder to the seam. The solder will melt and flow around the seam. If necessary, apply additional heat and solder. Be careful not to apply too much solder. When the solder has flowed completely

around the seam, let the object cool until the solder hardens before removing it from the soldering bench.

SOFT SOLDERING HINTS

A soldering copper is not recommended for art metal work for the process is slow and the copper leaves too much solder outside the seam.

When two large pieces are to be sweat soldered together, one piece is first tinned; that is, a thin layer of solder is melted onto its back. The two pieces are then clamped together and then heated until the solder remelts and fuses them.

When tinning the back of a large flat piece of metal first clean the metal, then apply the flux, and finally melt the solder onto the metal. While still fluid, the solder can be spread even and smoothly over the metal by rubbing with steel wool. A rag can be used instead of the steel wool.

Very small objects such as initials or thin wire work can be soft soldered to a larger piece by the following method: First melt a thin layer of solder onto a flat piece of scrap copper. The solder can be spread thin by rubbing with a rag or with fine steel wool. Now place the small objects, bottom side down, on the solder on the copper. Reheat

Fig. 26 Soft soldering with wire solder

the metal, the solder will remelt and stick to the bottom of the small objects, and while the solder is still liquid push the small objects off the copper with a steel rod. The small objects will have a thin layer of solder on their bottom side. Now place the small objects where desired and reheat to solder them permanently. Remember, a flux must be used.

It is not necessary to pickle (clean in acid) objects that have been soft soldered. The comparatively low heat (400° F.) required to melt soft solder will not oxidize the metals being soldered and therefore pickling is not required.

Greasy flux deposits, after soft soldering with fluxes such as No-Ko-Rode, can be removed with rags and fine steel wool. The flux is best removed by brushing the object with a jeweler's bristle brush or even an old tooth brush in a hot water solution of a yellow soap and a few drops of ammonia. Several of the new household detergents also can be used.

Beginner's Error. The greatest error beginners make when soft soldering is to overheat the metal thus causing the flux to turn black which prevents the solder from flowing and adhering. If this happens, the metal must be cooled and cleaned again.

PEWTER SOLDERING

Pewter is soldered with a soft solder. However, since the melting point (475° F.) of modern pewter is close to the lowest melting soft solder (356° F.) one must be careful when soldering pewter for if the metal is overheated slightly it melts quickly. It is best when soldering pewter to use a soft flame which is obtained by using less air with the blowpipe or torch. It is also best to move the flame continuously to avoid overheating the metal. By observing the above two precautions and by rechecking the other soft solder suggestions, one should develop the ability to soft solder pewter quickly.

Some craftsmen prefer to use bismuth soft solder (an alloy of bismuth, tin, and lead) which has an approximate melting point of

Fig. 26A Aluminum tray with soldered base

200° F. Glycerine, with 5 drops of muriatic acid to the ounce, is the preferred flux. No-Ko-Rode paste also is recommended.

ALUMINUM SOLDERING

Until comparatively recent years, thin sheet aluminum could not be soldered:— thick pieces were welded together. Recently, several companies have developed alloys for soldering aluminum. These alloys require different techniques so that one must follow the instructions accompanying the solders.

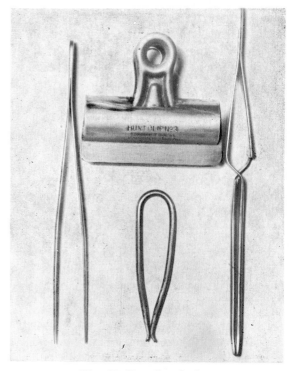
Fig. 27 Clamping devices

The solders do not flow as the soft and hard solders do, and the different color of the solder can be objectionable. However, they do permit the craftsmen to use, design, and assemble many additional craft and commercial objects in aluminum. It is hoped that improvements will still be made in the aluminum solders.

Caution: Aluminum has a comparatively low melting point (1220° F.) so that one must be careful not to overheat and thus melt the metal when soldering.

CLAMPING DEVICES

Where possible use binding wire, clamps, or soldering tweezers to hold metals in position while soldering. The wire (18 to 22 gauge) is tightened by twisting with a flat nose plier and by pulling out with the plier while twisting. Small clamps can be made from 1/16" or ⅛" steel wire by flattening ends and then bending to shape shown in figure 27. Cotter pins can also be used. Cross locking soldering tweezers (fig. 27) are highly recommended as clamps for both soft and hard soldering operations. Spring clamps (fig. 27) can be used only for soft soldering.

2. PICKLING

Copper and alloy metals containing copper oxidize when heated. The oxide formed is copper oxide. It is black and undesirable, and must be removed. In other words, when a copper or sterling silver object is hard soldered, the heat oxidizes the copper or the copper in the sterling silver alloy and, therefore, the object becomes black. The black oxide is generally called fire scale.

Pickling is the name given to the process of removing the oxide by means of acid.

For silver and gold the following solution is used:

Water, 10 parts; Sulfuric Acid, 1 part.

Heating speeds the pickling action of the solution and the solution is most effective when boiled.

The pickling solution, with jewelry or

Fig. 28 Pickling Pan

small silver objects in it, can be boiled in a copper pickle pan (fig. 28); pyrex and ceramic crucibles can also be used. The pickling solution for large silver objects can be heated in a pyrex pan or in a lead container or earthenware crock. After using, the hot solution is poured back into its container so that it can be reused. The metal objects are washed with water to remove all traces of acid. Copper, brass, bronze, and nickel silver are pickled in a solution of:

Water, 5 parts; Nitric Acid, 1 part.

The solution is generally used cold and the objects to be pickled are left in it for a minute or two, removed and washed with water. The hot sulfuric acid can also be used.

The pickling solutions, besides removing the oxide from the metal, also dissolve the hardened glazed flux so that the metal can better be worked and observed.

The pickling solution can be kept in an earthenware crock (fig. 29). Small quantities can be stored in glass containers.

CAUTION When preparing a pickling solution, first pour the water into the container and then add the acid (fig. 30). If water is poured into concentrated acid, the acid is apt

Fig. 29 Earthenware Crock

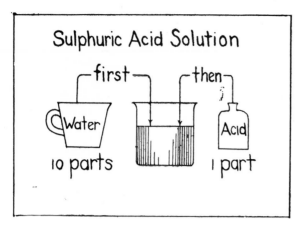

Fig. 30 Method of preparing pickling solution

to splash. Acid burns should be washed with water immediately and neutralized with bicarbonate of soda or soap.

Sparex No. 2, a commercial preparation, can also be used for pickling. Though slower in action than acid and a little more expensive, Sparex has the advantage of being less corrosive, and is therefore recommended for schools, and also commercial establishments where ventilation is poor.

Note: Always remove binding wire from objects before pickling; otherwise, the objects become coated with a thin layer of copper. Immerse and remove objects with copper wire or copper tweezers. **Reminder:** — soft soldered objects do not have to be pickled.

OXIDATION PREVENTION Pickling in sulfuric acid does not remove the fire scale (formed when hard soldering) from sterling silver; it merely deposits a silvery finish on the top surface. After pickling, when the object is polished, the silvery finish is removed, exposing the fire scale which now has a dull grayish color. The scale can be completely removed by time-consuming polishing or it can be prevented before soldering or removed by acids as explained below.

BORIC ACID SOLUTION A saturated solution of boric acid is made by dropping an excessive amount of boric acid in boiling water. Silver objects are warmed slightly and dipped into the solution. The boric acid that adheres to the solution will prevent the formation of the fire scale.

BORIC ACID AND ALCOHOL This can be used for small gold and silver objects. Boric acid is mixed with alcohol and kept in a covered jar. The metal object is dropped into the solution, removed, heated to ignite and remove the alcohol, thus leaving a thin coating of boric acid.

If formed, fire scale (copper oxide) can be removed from silver by immersing the silver into a cold 50% water and 50% nitric acid solution. The solution is very strong and the object must be removed quickly. It is best not to use the above unless absolutely necessary.

Most commercial silversmiths remove the fire scale from silver by polishing with pumice. Tripoli polishing (page 37) also will remove the fire scale.

3. ANNEALING

Metals when worked, that is when hammer formed, drawn into a wire, rolled, or bent, become hard and brittle, so much so that with further working they will crack. Annealing, the term for softening metals by heat, is done by heating the metals. The temperature to which the metal is heated and the methods of cooling varies with different metals.

Scientifically speaking, metals become soft

Fig. 31 Annealing a silver bowl

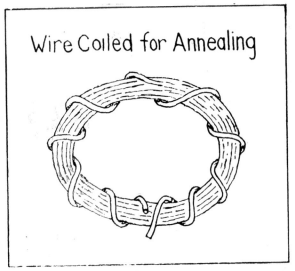

Fig. 32

at certain temperatures because the grain structure of the metal changes (recrystalization occurs).

The following should be observed when annealing:

No solder, especially soft, should be in contact with the metal for the solder will burn into it.

Objects that have hard soldered parts must be annealed at a temperature below the melting point of the solder.

All parts of the metal must be heated, though on large pieces not necessarily all over at the same time.

Do not drop sterling silver or brass into cold water when red hot for they are liable to crack.

STERLING SILVER Sterling Silver is heated to a very light red (first red, 900° F., will do), permitted to cool to lose its redness, and then it may be dropped into water so that it may be handled quickly. It is best, however, in order to avoid warping effects of sudden cooling, to permit large formed objects to cool slowly to room temperature.

COPPER Copper is heated to light red heat and then dipped immediately into water, though it may be permitted to cool slowly in air.

BRASS Brass is heated to light red, cooled until the redness disappears, otherwise it may crack. It is then dipped into water.

ALUMINUM Aluminum is heated until a piece of wood when rubbed on it will char. If aluminum is heated to red heat, it will melt since its melting point is only 1220° F.

STEEL Steel is heated to cherry red and permitted to cool as slowly as possible in air or, better yet, powdered asbestos.

PEWTER Pewter remains soft and after being worked does not have to be annealed.

GOLD Gold, yellow and green, is heated to a dull red (1200° F.) and white gold is heated to cherry red (1400° F.). They are permitted to cool slightly and then may be dipped into water. Red gold is heated to dull red and then dipped immediately into water.

WIRE Wire, especially very thin sterling, is coiled as shown in figure 32 in order to avoid melting. Note that the ends of the wire are wrapped around the coil to hold it together. Use a soft, almost yellow flame when annealing: that is—a flame with very little air.

4. SHEARS AND THEIR USES

Hand shears and snips are available in several shapes and lengths. The following are recommended:

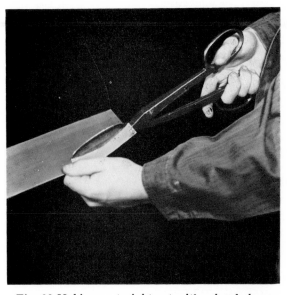

Fig. 33 Making a straight cut with a hand shear

12″ tinners' hand snips, straight blade, for craftsmen.

10″ tinners' hand snips, straight blade, for schools.

7″ plate shears, plain handle, curved blade.

With the above, practically all required silversmithing and art metal hand cutting operations can be accomplished efficiently. Compound lever shears, universal metal shears, aviation, and silversmith's shears, are popular with individual craftsmen. A foot squaring shear is very desirable, especially in a school shop.

CUTTING OPERATIONS

STRAIGHT CUTS Straight cuts on metals up to 16 gauge are made with a hand shear with a straight blade (fig. 33). For easy cutting, the metal is held as near to the pivot point of the jaws of the shears as possible and also straight out or perpendicular to the jaws. For long straight cuts, the metal is constantly pushed into the jaws of the shears as the cutting proceeds.

CIRCLES The circle is cut from a square piece of metal with a hand shear with a straight blade as follows: First, lines are drawn from the corners of the square piece of metal to locate its center. A divider is used to swing the circle. The corners of the square are then cut off fairly close to the circle to form an octagon. By holding the metal perpendicular to the shears (fig. 33A) and as close to the pivot point as possible, it is now very easy to cut the circle.

CONCAVE CUTS The 7″ plate shears with curved blade is used for making all types of concave cuts. A good quality plate shear is a sturdy cutting tool that can easily cut 18 gauge metal.

TRIMMING EDGES The edges of bowls and vases can be trimmed with the 7″ plate shear. When using the plate shear for trimming purposes, it is best that the curved blade point out, not in, as shown in fig. 34.

HACK SAWS The hack saw (fig. 35) can be used for cutting large tubes, heavy bars, and

Fig. 33A Cutting a circle with a straight shear

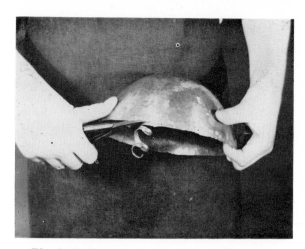

Fig. 34 Trimming an edge with a plate shear

Fig. 35 Cutting a brass bar with a hack saw

thick metals. 8″ hack saw blades with fine teeth (24 teeth per inch) are suggested for most required jobs. Suggestions when using a hack saw:—

The teeth of the blade point away from the handle.

Hold the frame with both hands.

Cut the metal with a steady (50 to 80 strokes per minute) even stroke.

5. THE JEWELER'S SAW AND BLADES

PURCHASING Saw frames can be purchased with different depths, ranging from 2¼″ up to 12″. The following are recommended:

A 4″ frame for general craft work.

A 10″ or 12″ frame for piercing (cutting inside the metal) large pieces of metal.

The 2¼″ frame is used by commercial gold and platinum jewelers.

Jeweler's saw blades can be purchased in sizes from 8/0, the thinnest, to number 14, the thickest. The size number, thickness, and width of the blades are shown in figure 36. Jeweler's saw blades are 5″ long.

The following saw blades are recommended:

Numbers 0 or 2 for general craft work.

Number 2/0 for piercing thin metals.

The thinner blades (3/0, 4/0) are used by gold and platinum jewelers.

The thicker blades are rarely used for hand sawing.

The blades are made from a good grade of tool steel. Rarely will a quality blade wear out. They usually break from misuse.

HOW TO INSERT BLADE Hold the frame as shown in figure 37. Insert the blade in the front (top) of the frame. The teeth of the blade should point out and down towards the handle. Tighten the wing screw to lock the blade in position. If necessary, adjust the length of the frame so that the blade extends to about the center of the lower jaws. Press the handle in with your hand or chest. Insert the blade between the jaws and, while still pressing the frame in, tighten the jaws

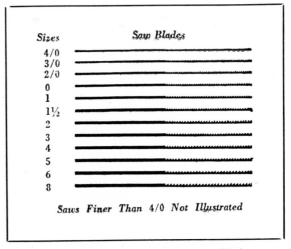

Fig. 36 Sizes of Jeweler's saw blades

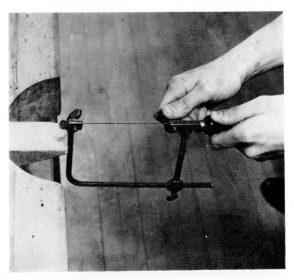

Fig. 37 Inserting the saw blade

Fig. 38 Bench pin for a school shop

31

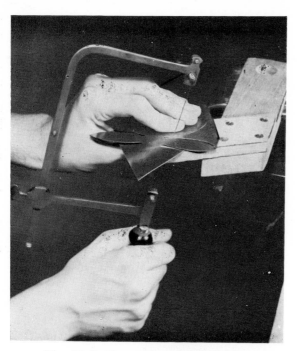

Fig. 39 Cutting with a Jeweler's saw

by means of the wing screw. This operation will leave the blade very taut and a taut blade is essential for proper cutting.

Tighten the wing screw by hand only. The use of a plier should be avoided since it is slow and tends to damage the threads of the wing screw.

SAWING PROCEDURE The sawing operation is fairly easy. Long, even strokes are the best. Very little forward pressure is required. Incline the saw frame forward about five degrees (fig. 39), no more, for general cutting. To make a perfect right angle cut, hold the saw perpendicular and, without pressing forward, make a series of light cuts, each time turning the saw frame or work slightly until the right angle cut has been made. Saw as close to the line of the design as possible, not directly on it but slightly outside towards the waste material. After the sawing has been completed, the line of the design is used as a guide for filing. Accurate sawing, however, calls for very little filing. A very taut blade, if used on its side, can be used as a file when doing fine piercing.

When piercing, that is—cutting a design inside the metal, a very small hole is drilled

through the metal. The blade is inserted through the hole and then tightened so that the necessary cutting can be made.

Some metal workers, not all, prefer to add bee's wax to the saw blade when cutting. A piece of bee's wax is pressed against the side of the bench pin and the blade is touched to it occasionally.

It is best to saw the metal on a bench pin —which is a piece of wood with a "V" cut into it (fig. 38). This way the work can be held by hand and it and the saw can be manipulated for fast accurate cutting. Very small objects can be held with a "Bernard" type plier, with the plier pressed against the bench pin.

A professional jeweler's (fig. 2) work bench (used by metal workers too) has a bench pin inserted (by means of a mortise and tenon joint) into the front of the bench —an ideal arrangement. The bench pin in figure 38 is recommended for school shops for it can be clamped in a vise, wood or machinist, and then hung on the side of the bench when not used.

Caution:—Beginners should avoid clamping the metal to be sawed to the bench pin, table, or vise since the clamping takes time and also does not permit proper manipulation of the metal.

If a saw cut must be made on a long piece of metal and if the saw frame isn't long enough but is sufficiently wide for the cut, the saw blade can be inserted sidewards in the frame as follows. Heat the ends, about 1/2", of the saw blade until light red and then permit to cool slowly in air. This will soften them. Then, with a flat nose plier, bend the ends of the blade until a right angle is formed. Now the blade can be inserted sidewards in the frame so that the long saw cut can be made.

6. FILES AND FILING TECHNIQUES

MAKES Files may be divided into two classifications or patterns—Swiss and American. The Swiss pattern files are considered superior for silversmithing and jewelry work. The coarseness of a Swiss file is marked by a number. Number 00 is the coarsest and, becoming progressively smoother, the other files are numbered 0, 1, 2, up to 8. Rarely is a file finer than number 4 required for silversmithing and art metal work. Recommended:—number 0 for rough quick filing, number 2 for most filing, number 4 for finish filing.

The coarseness or fineness of American pattern files is specified by name. Rough, bastard, second cut, smooth, and super smooth are the standard cuts.

Though the Swiss files are more expensive than the American their additional cost is warranted for professional work. Several American firms are now making Swiss pattern files for silversmiths and jewelers.

CUTS Single, double, vixen, and rasp are common cuts of files. Single cut files have a single row of parallel teeth running the entire length of the file. The teeth are slanted at an angle of 65 to 85 degrees to the edge of the file (fig. 40). Single cut files are the only files that can be used for draw filing (described later) and when so used they finish the metal smoother than other cut files of a similar fineness. The American pattern mill file is a single cut file and so are files for sharpening saws.

Double cut files have an additional row of teeth cut at an angle of 60 degrees to the first row. Double cut files remove metal faster than single cut files of a similar coarse-

ness. Swiss pattern files are double cut and so are most American pattern files.

Vixen cut files have a single row of curved teeth running across the file for its entire length. Rasp cut files have short, raised teeth that are spaced at even intervals over the cutting length of the file. Rasp and vixen files are used on soft metals like lead, aluminum, pewter, and on wood and plastics.

SHAPES Files can be purchased in many geometric cross-sectional shapes. Some of the popular shapes are shown in figure 40. Recommended for most silversmithing and art metal work: half-round and flat hand files.

NEEDLE FILES Needle files are especially adapted for file finishing small and delicate objects. A popular size is the 16 centimeter, which has an overall length of 5½" and a cutting length of 2¾". Note (fig. 40) that the round end of the needle file forms its handle. The files are sold individually or in a set of 12—all of a different shape. Recommended: half-round, three corner, and barrette.

RIFFLER FILES Riffler or die sinker's files are tool steel rods with a very small file on both ends. Silversmith rifflers are similar to the above in shape but have larger and wider file surfaces. Rifflers are available with many curved and odd shaped surfaces.

With the introduction of the flexible shaft (fig. 8A) the need for riffler files by most metal workers has diminished for with the small grinding and polishing wheels available for the shaft it is now possible to get to surfaces formerly only possible with riffler files.

FILING TECHNIQUES

Accurate and rapid filing is best accomplished on most silver and art metal objects by holding the object to be filed against the work bench or bench pin (fig. 41). Avoid the use of a vise.

When filing, use the entire cutting length of the file where necessary.

Use a rough file to remove metal quickly and a fine file for finishing.

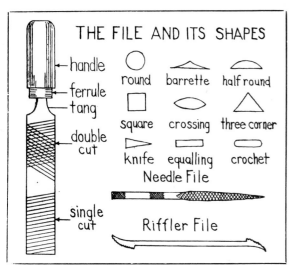

Fig. 40 File terminology

Files cut on the forward stroke only. Reduce your pressure on the file if you do not lift it when you draw it back.

On long narrow edges, as the file is pushed, it is also moved sidewards to get even, smooth edges that are free of grooves.

Small objects can be held while being filed with pliers or a ring clamp. However, when possible, it is best to hold the objects by hand and the hand or object should rest on the bent pin for quick, accurate filing. A properly used bench pin becomes well grooved from the edge of the file and eventually must be replaced.

When filing, occasionally tap the file on the bench pin to remove particles of metal that may stick to the file's teeth. A file card or cleaner, which is a steel wire brush, can also be used for removing metals from files.

TO FILE THE EDGE OF A BOWL Place the bowl so that its top edge rests on the work bench's edge or on a bench pin (fig. 41). Hold the file so that it is perpendicular to the edge of the bowl. Push the file forward, press as hard as you can against it, and while so doing also push it sidewards to the left or right. After part of the edge of the bowl has been filed, rotate the bowl and then repeat the filing operation until the entire edge has been filed. Start with a rough

Fig. 42 Filing a scalloped edge

file, then use a smoother file; finally, complete the operation with emery paper.

TO FILE A SCALLOPED EDGE ON A BOWL Rest the edge of the bowl on the edge of a work bench or bench pin. Use a half round or barrette file. File each edge of the scallop separately. Place the file, flat side down, at the bottom of the scallop and perpendicular to the edge of one of the sides. Push the file forward and at the same time sidewards to the outer edge (fig. 42). This will smooth the edge of the metal and also form a pleasant curved scallop. Repeat the filing operation for the other side of the scallop.

If a deep scallop is required, before filing, some of the metal can be removed with the 7 inch curved plate shears.

DRAW FILING Long, straight, wide edges of metal can be draw filed to a smooth finish. A single cut smooth file must be used. The metal is held in a vise and if necessary the metal's surface is protected by copper safety jaws. Hold the file with two hands, perpendicular and also at a right angle to the edge of the metal to be draw filed. Apply a firm pressure to the file and then draw it back and forth across the entire edge of the

Fig. 41 Filing the edge of a bowl

metal to be draw filed. This will, due to a shearing action of the file teeth, leave the metal very smooth. **Note:** It is important when draw filing not to rock the file but to hold it perfectly perpendicular to the metal in order to obtain a truly flat and smooth surface.

7. EMERY AND ITS USES

Art metal and silver objects, after they are filed and before they are polished, are rubbed with emery to remove all file marks and scratches. Emery is a natural form of aluminum oxide mixed with iron oxide. It can be purchased as a powder or gritted, or glued to paper or cloth, or imbedded in rubber. All types are used by art metal workers and silversmiths.

Emery paper and cloth are graded by numbers as follows: 4/0 (the finest), 3/0, 2/0, 1/0, $\frac{1}{2}$, 1, $1\frac{1}{2}$, 2 and 3 (the coarsest). Numbers $\frac{1}{2}$ to 2 are recommended for removing file marks and fine scratches from metals so that they can be polished. Emery paper is suggested, not cloth, for most work since it can be used to make an emery stick (described below) and since it is less expensive. Some metal workers prefer the cloth for polishing stakes and for rubbing planished surfaces in-

Fig. 44 Rolling emery onto a muslin wheel

order to better observe the hammer marks.

Emery powder (flour) and grit are graded as follows: powder sizes are FFF (the finest) FF, F. Grit sizes are 240 (the finest) 220, 180, 150, 120, 100, 80, 60. 180 and 240 grit and FF powder are sufficient for most craft work.

Ways of using commercial emery products and attachments that can be purchased or made are described below.

EMERY STICK Emery paper can be used similarly to a file by wrapping it around a piece of wood 3/16 x 1 x 12 inches (fig. 43). This is best done by laying the emery paper with the emery side down on a bench. Then, with a knife or sharp edge of a barrette file, score the paper where it is to be bent around the stick. Wrap the paper around the stick and repeat the process until the entire sheet of emery is wrapped firmly around the stick. The scoring of the paper will give it sharp edges where it is bent. The end of the emery paper is tacked to the narrow side of the stick or it can be held to the stick by means of binding wire on both ends. As the paper wears down, rip off the top layer and use the one beneath.

EMERY WHEELS — GLUED FLEXIBLE TYPE Emery wheels, the glued flexible type, are excellent for quickly removing scratches and file marks from stakes, hammers, and metal objects. The wheels are made by glu-

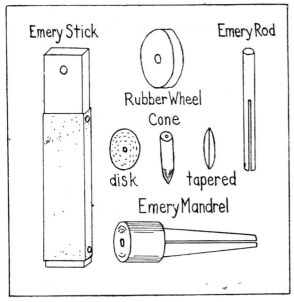

Emery Stick

Emery Rod

Rubber Wheel

Cone

disk   tapered

Emery Mandrel

Fig. 43

ing emery, powdered or grit to muslin buffs, 4" and larger in diameter. These wheels, when used, will give slightly, due to the muslin core, and will tend to match the contour of the metal surface being polished and leave a smooth finish; whereas, a solid emery wheel (grindstone type) will cut into the metal.

The emery is glued to the muslin wheels as follows: Place a large nail or rod through the center of the wheel. With a brush, apply glue to the circumference or outer edge of the muslin wheel. While the glue is still wet roll the wheel through the emery which has previously been spread over newspaper (fig. 44). The emery will stick to the glue. Now roll the wheel over clean newspaper until the emery deposited on it is even. Permit the glue to harden overnight before using the wheel.

Note: Freshly prepared woodworker's hot flake (fish) glue is used as the glue. The wheels should receive the emery in a moderately warm room, not cold, so that the glue will not become chilled and thus harden too quickly.

When used, the emery wheels first should be broken in (trued) by holding a piece of steel (an old file will do) against them while they revolve. The metal object being emeried must be moved continuously to obtain a smooth surface free of grooves. Use a rough emery wheel first and finish emerying with a finer grit or emery flour flexible muslin wheel. Wax and even tripoli can be applied to the emery wheels to obtain a smoother finish.

Safety precaution: — wear safety goggles when using the emery wheel.

EMERY ROD Fine emery paper can be wrapped around a $\frac{1}{8}$" rod held in the chuck of a flexible shaft outfit and then it can be used to remove scratches from flat and concave flat surfaces. The rod, brass preferred, is made by slotting its length from 1 to 2 inches with a jeweler's saw (fig. 43). The end of a strip of emery paper 2 to 3 inches long is inserted in the rod and then the rest

of the paper is wrapped around the rod counter-clockwise. It is then used where desired.

EMERY MANDREL The emery mandrel (fig. 43) is used to smooth the inside of rings and bands. The end of the mandrel screws onto the tapered spindle of the polishing machine. The end of a strip of emery paper is inserted into the slot in the mandrel so that it can be used.

RUBBER WHEELS Small rubber wheels ($\frac{1}{4}$" to $\frac{1}{2}$" dia.) mixed with emery are available for the flexible shaft outfit. The wheels are excellent for removing scratches from crevices and other places which are not accessible to files. A rubber wheel can be shaped by holding a file against it while it revolves.

EMERY DISKS AND WHEELS Small emery disks and wheels, similar to the types used by dentists, are available for use with a flexible shaft outfit.

SCOTCH STONE Scotch stone, a natural abrasive, was once popular with craftsmen for removing scratches. It has been supplanted by the disks described above or, where a flexible shaft is not available, by emery imbedded rubber tablets or sticks which are used by hand.

ROUGE AND CROCUS PAPER Rouge and crocus paper are used by craftsmen to get fine satin and polished hand finishes.

8. POLISHING AND BUFFING

Polishing is a cutting action; metal is removed by an abrasive. Buffing is a combination of a cutting and burnishing action; some metal is removed but most is burnished to a high bright finish.

THE POLISHING AND BUFFING COMPOUNDS Tripoli and rouge are the two standard compounds used by craftsmen. Tripoli is a silicon substance (diatomaceous

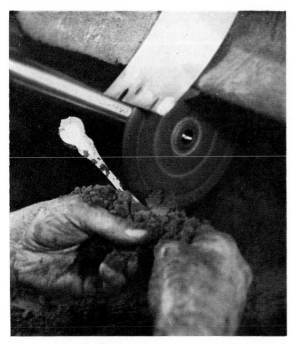

Fig. 45 Silver spoon being pumiced

earth); rouge is a fine iron oxide. Both are mixed with grease to form bars or cakes which are convenient to handle and apply to the buffing wheels.

Tripoli is a fast cutting abrasive compound which is used to remove emery marks and fine scratches. When used properly, it leaves the metal very smooth but still dull in appearance.

Rouge produces the final high color or luster and it does this primarily by burnishing the metal. By means of the rouge, high surface speed, and heat caused by friction the metal actually flows to fill in minute scratches, thus producing the final lustrous coloring.

Pumice is used by commercial silversmiths as a fast cutting abrasive to prepare silver objects for tripoli and then rouge.

It is a porous and fibrous volcanic lava, which is grayish-white in color. Pumice can be purchased in lump form, as a powder, or in the form of a cake.

Lump pumice is used with water to remove scratches from flat metal surfaces. When used, water is applied to the metal and then the lump pumice is rubbed back and forth until the deep scratches are removed.

Powdered pumice is mixed with a com-bination of light machine oil and water to hold it together. When used, it is thrown up and onto the revolving polishing wheel (fig. 45) or it is fed to the revolving wheel by permitting it to slide down the metal object being polished. A pan beneath the polishing wheel is required to hold and to catch the pumice. Powdered pumice is graded and can be purchased as follows: extra coarse-2, coarse-1, medium-½, fine-2/0. Bobbing compound is the commercial name for powdered pumice held together in cake form by means of a grease binder.

POLISHING AND BUFFING WHEELS— Craftsmen and schools use 5 and 6 inch diameter wheels for polishing and buffing art metal and silverware objects. Larger wheels, 8, 10, 12, or 14 inch, are preferred by commercial polishers. Smaller wheels, 2, 3, or 4 inch are recommended for small and delicate objects. Generally, the harder, close stitched wheels are used with tripoli for fast cutting; the softer, loose stitched or unstitched wheels are used with rouge. Muslin wheels are used with tripoli; flannel wheels with rouge.

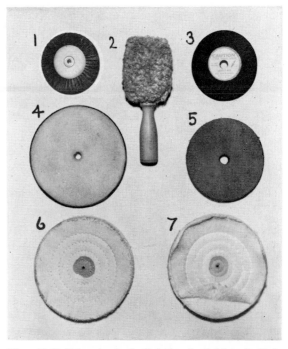

Fig. 46 Polish wheels 1. Bristle, 2. Goblet, 3. Rubber, 4. Felt, 5. Walrus, 6. Muslin, 7. Cotton flannel

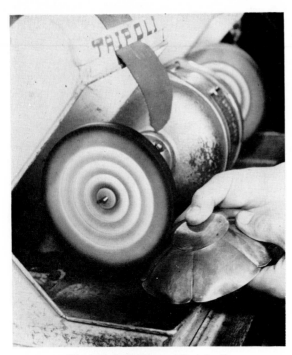

Fig. 47 Polishing with tripoli

Bristle wheels are used to get into corners and crevices not accessible to muslin or flannel wheels.

Walrus wheels, made from walrus leather, is preferred for pumice polishing since it is a tough, porous leather which holds the pumice for fast polishing. The wheels should be soaked in neats foot oil, drained, and then hammered to soften evenly.

Felt wheels, especially the hard ones, since they do not give, can be used to maintain sharp corners on metal objects. They also can be used with pumice.

The inside of cups, pitchers, vases, etc., can be polished with cylinders or tapered buffs or by goblets (fig. 46). The above are available in muslin, cotton, and bristle.

Brass wire scratch brushes are used to impart a satin finish to silver, copper, and other metals.

Sheepskin buffs are popular for buffing soft metals such as Britannia or pewter.

TRUMMING The inner surface of pierced objects and inaccessible areas around spouts and handles can be polished with cord or flannel or cotton rags. The cord is used for fine pierced objects and the rags are used around the handles, spouts and other inaccessible spots.

When trumming, one end of the cord or rag is held in a vise and the other end in one's hand. The polishing compound is rubbed onto the cord or rag and then the object to be polished is rubbed back and forth over the cord or rags until the desired results are obtained.

CLEANING PROCEDURE Cleanliness is essential for successful polishing. It should be apparent that the wheels must be used with one compound only and that they should not be contaminated by other compounds. In large commercial concerns separate machines are used for pumice, tripoli, and rouge.

If objects have been hard soldered, they must be pickled before being polished. After using tripoli and before buffing with rouge, objects should be cleaned in a hot water solution of soap and a few drops of ammonia. A jeweler's bristle brush is used to wash out the tripoli from crevices and corners. An old tooth brush can be used for small objects.

The same cleaning procedure as above should be used after rouge buffing. Chamois skins or prepared polishing cloths can be used to handle objects after they have been polished and washed.

POLISHING AND BUFFING TECHNIQUES

1. It is faster and better to remove deep scratches with a file and file marks with emery paper than it is to attempt to remove them by polishing.

2. Fine emery marks are removed from the metal by polishing with tripoli (or pumice) and all marks should be removed before the metal is buffed with rouge.

3. It takes longer to tripoli an object than it does to rouge it. Spend 90% of the finishing time on the tripoli wheel.

4. The top of the polishing wheel must turn towards the operator. The objects to be polished are held below the horizontal center line of the wheel in the position shown in figure 48.

5. Press the object firmly (as hard as possible) against the revolving polishing wheel.

6. Avoid holding objects too long in one position, otherwise undesirable grooves may be formed. It is best to turn or move the metal continuously while polishing.

7. Chains are best polished on a flat piece of wood around which the chains may be wrapped. A nail or hook may be attached to the wood to hold one end of the chain.

8. Cleanliness is important. Wash the object after using the tripoli and rouge in a hot water and soap solution and a few drops of ammonia.

9. CHEMICAL FINISHES

The external surface of metal objects can be treated with chemicals in order to obtain several practical and interesting finishes. Below are several popular chemical finishes used by craftsmen.

Objects to be treated are first polished with tripoli and rouge; however, much craft work may be prepared for the chemicals merely by rubbing with fine emery cloth, steel wool, or by wire brushing.

Cleanliness is essential. After polishing, remove all traces of the polishing compounds by brushing the objects in a hot water and soap solution that has a few drops of ammonia added to it.

Antique (bluish-black) Finish on Silver and Copper The chemical used is potassium sul-phide, commonly called liver of sulphur. The solution, the most popular and also the easiest to prepare, is made by dropping a ½″ cube of the chemical into a quart of hot water. A small object may be dropped into the solution and removed when it turns bluish-black. If the finish did not take in spots, clean those spots with steel wool and return object to the solution. The finish can be applied to a large object by dipping steel wool into the solution and then by rubbing the solution and thus the finish onto the object by means of the steel wool.

When the desired color has been obtained, wipe the object with a soft rag until it is dry. Then with dry, fine steel wool, pumice powder, or on the buffing machine, tone the object where desired to obtain bright contrasting effects.

Note:—It is often advisable, especially in school shops, to make a concentrated liquid solution of potassium sulphide by dropping large pieces of the solid chemical (potassium sulphide) into a bottle or jar (which can be capped) of warm water. When a usable solution is desired, pour some of the concentrated solution into hot water.

Red to Purple to Black on Copper In one quart of water, dissolve 2 ounces of sodium hyposulphite and 1 ounce of lead acetate; then boil. Immerse the copper until the desired color appears.

Blue to Black on Brass or Nickel Silver The above may be used. Brass immersed in a boiling solution of butter of antimony (antimony trichloride) will turn black.

Black on Silver, Gold, Copper and Its Alloys Dissolve I ounce of tellurium dioxide in ½ pint of hydrochloric acid, then dilute with water. Dilute with 2 parts of water for silver and gold; six parts of water for copper, brass, and nickel silver. If the solution is too strong, the black color will peel off the copper.

Objects may be dipped into the solution or the solution may be brushed onto the object with an old tooth brush. Caution should be used in handling and preparing the solution since it contains hydrochloric acid.

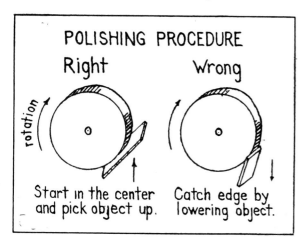

POLISHING PROCEDURE

Right | Wrong

rotation

Start in the center and pick object up. | Catch edge by lowering object.

Fig. 48

GREEN ON COPPER For a contrasting effect, a dark liver of sulphur finish is usually first applied to the copper; then the green solution is brushed or stippled on. The brushing or stippling may be repeated. When the desired effect is obtained, the object can be sprayed with lacquer. After lacquering, a semi-glossy appearance may be produced by applying beeswax or carnauba wax to a soft wheel and then polishing the object lightly.

Tiffany Green

Copper sulfate	8 oz.
Ammonium chloride	4 oz.
Sodium chloride	1 oz.
Zinc chloride	2 oz.
Acetic acid	2 oz.
Water	1 gal.

Antique Green

Copper nitrate	4 oz.
Ammonium chloride	4 oz.
Calcium chloride	4 oz.
Water	1/2 gal.

Dry colors such as chrome green, burnt sienna, ivory white, black, Indian red, added to the solution also will produce interesting effects.

10. DRILLS AND DRILLING

SIZES Drills are sized several ways: by numbers, fractions, letters, or metrically. The number system is the one used most often by silversmiths and jewelers. The drills in the number system run from number one, the largest, to number eighty, the smallest. Below is listed different sized drills and their equivalents in thousandths of an inch.

80	.013	60	.040	35	.110
1/64	.015	55	.052	1/8	.125
75	.021	1/16	.062	30	.128
70	.028	50	.070	15	.180
1/32	.031	45	.082	1	.228
65	.035	40	.098	1/4	.250

CENTER PUNCHING To assure that the drill enters the metal where desired, the exact spot to be drilled must be centerpunched or marked. This may be done several ways: with a spring or regular center punch, an awl, or an engraving tool. The spring center punch is pressed or the regular punch is tapped at the desired position. The awl is pressed firmly and rotated slightly where the hole is to be drilled. The engraving tool, a diamond or lozenge one, is rotated where desired to form the mark for the drill.

DRILLING METHODS Holes may be drilled by means of a hand drill, a drill press, or a flexible shaft outfit.

To insert a drill in a hand drill, place it in the hand drill's chuck. Hold the chuck firmly with one hand and with the other hand turn the handle of the hand drill clockwise to tighten the jaws of the chuck around the drill.

To drill a hole, place the drill in the center punch mark, press down on the knob of the hand drill, then turn the crank clockwise. When drilling with a drill as small as number 60, care must be taken not to press down too hard in order to avoid breaking the drill.

With a drill press, holes can be drilled quickly, accurately, and with less effort. For most drilling operations, the rotating drill, by means of a lever, is pressed down against

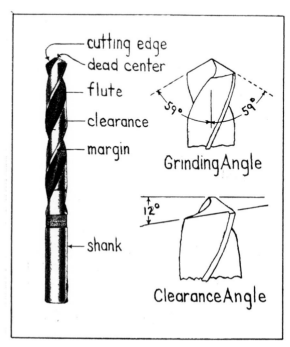

Fig. 49 A twist drill and its cutting angles

and through the metal to be drilled. The following drilling method permits one to drill small holes (numbers 60 to 80) through flat metals with less drill breakage and through curved objects that would be difficult to drill otherwise with a drill press. Lock the drill in the chuck of the drill press. Hold the object to be drilled in one's hand and press the object up against the rotating drill until the hole is drilled.

A flexible shaft outfit (fig. 8A) is indispensable for professional jewelry work and very desirable for most silversmithing and art metal work. With it, one may remain seated at the work bench while drilling small holes. The accuracy, speed, and versatility of a flexible shaft outfit more than repays its initial cost in a short time.

DRILLING HINTS The drill or metal must be oiled often while drilling. Oil keeps the drill cool and sharp. A light machine oil or cutting oil is best.

Thin drills should protrude from the drill chuck as little as possible since they tend to snap easily. Often the shank of a drill must be snapped off so that the drill will not stick out too much.

Use higher speed for smaller drills than for larger (wider) ones. However, the pressure applied (feed) must be less to avoid snapping the drill. Small drills tend to snap when they break through the back of the metal being drilled. Carbon steel drills are superior for drilling through thin sheets of copper and silver since they do not snap as easily. High speed drills are superior for drilling steel.

SHARPENING DRILLS Drills eventually become dull and must be resharpened. They may be sharpened several ways:—namely, by means of the grindstone, oilstone, or flexible shaft.

Note, from figure 49, the following:

1. The drill turns clockwise.
2. The actual cutting (drilling) is done at two cutting edges, the lips.
3. The twisted flute helps to form the cutting edge. It also removes the metal being cut, curls the chip tightly within it-

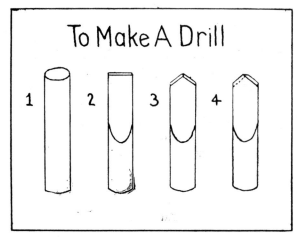

To Make A Drill

1   2   3   4

Fig. 50

self, and permits the oil to get down to the cutting edges.

4. The surface of the "point" is ground away from the lips at a 12 degree angle to give the lips a real cutting edge.
5. The angle of the lips (in relation to the axis of the drill) should be equal; 59 degrees is recommended for most work.
6. Both lips should be of the same length.

GRINDSTONE METHOD Drills that are larger than number 50 are best sharpened on an electric grindstone. Each lip is sharpened separately. The drill is held against the stone so that the lip forms the required 59° angle with the axis of the drill. Then, while grinding the 59° angle with the axis of the drill, the drill is twisted slightly to form the 12° lip clearance angle. Study the shape of a new drill. With a little practice, it should be easy to grind the drill properly.

OILSTONE METHOD The drill, held in a pin vise, is rubbed on a hard arkansas stone. First adjust the pin vise to obtain the 59° angle on one of the lips and then incline the vise for the 12° angle. Sharpen the other lip the same way. The oilstone may be rubbed against the drill.

FLEXIBLE SHAFT METHOD This method is very easy with small drills. The drill is held in a pin vise. A small, flat emery wheel (3/4" dia. x 1/8" wide will do) is placed in the chuck of the flexible shaft. The drill is held against the rotating emery wheel at the proper angles. With a little practice and study, drills can be sharpened very quickly and accurately this way.

HOW TO MAKE A SMALL DRILL (fig. 50)
It is comparatively easy to make a small drill if a manufactured one is not available. A sewing needle or any good grade of tool steel rod is required. The rod is first ground, as shown in the diagram, to a screw driver point. Then the 59° lip clearance angle is ground to form each lip. The 12° lip clearance angle is ground to complete the grinding process. The drill, if drill rod is used, must be hardened and then tempered to dark brown. This drill, surprisingly practical, can be made in a few minutes.

PUNCHING HOLES Often it is easier to punch a small hole through a metal than it is to drill it. This is especially true on flat thin metal (up to 18 gauge) that is to be pierced (sawed) and where the punched hole is used for inserting the jeweler's saw. A sharply ground pointed pick or awl is used and the punching is best done over a lead block. Hammer the punch until the metal breaks through, then remove the tool and punch back lightly from the opposite side to enlarge the hole.

11. HARDENING AND TEMPERING STEEL

Tool steel is hardened by heating it until cherry red (approximately 1400°) and then dipping it very quickly into cold water. This makes the steel very hard but brittle. It must be heated again, that is—tempered, to remove some of the brittleness.

A chasing tool can be hardened and tempered as follows: Heat about one inch of the tip of the tool until it is cherry red and then quickly dip it into cold water. Move the tool around in the water so that it will always be in a cold section. This should make the tip very hard but also too brittle to be used. The tip can be tested for hardness with a file. If it can be filed it is too soft.

Now polish the tool with emery paper. It is tempered by heating the steel about 1½" behind the tip. The proper tempering temperature can be obtained by observing the oxidation colors which appear. These colors, caused by the oxidation of steel when heated, indicate different degrees of temperature. It has been found that the higher the temperature of the steel, the darker the oxidation color and the less brittle the steel is. Note the colors as they appear. First—a light straw, then in order, dark straw, dark brown, purple, blue, and finally steel gray. The proper tempering temperature for the chasing tool is approximately 460° F. At this temperature the steel is dark straw in color.

Note If the steel is overheated when tempering, that is if it turns brown or blue, the entire process must be repeated. To soften hardened steel, heat the steel to cherry red and permit it to cool slowly in air, or better yet, in powdered asbestos.

Temp...Color		Suggested Uses
420° F	Light Straw	Engraving tools, scrapers
460° F	Dark Straw	Chasing tools, punches
500° F	Dark Brown	Drills
540° F	Purple	Hammer heads
570° F	Blue	Knives, screw drivers
630° F	Black	Springs

GRINDING TOOLS When grinding a tool such as an engraving tool, the tool must be dipped constantly into cold water to avoid "burning" the steel. By burning is meant the appearance of a blue color on the steel. This color is formed by the heat generated by the friction of the grinding operation, and it indicates that the steel has been tempered or softened too much. The tool will have to be hardened and then tempered to restore its original cutting properties.

The preferred grinding wheel is a soft emery or soap stone one and the wheels should be mounted on an electric machine.

SUGGESTIONS WHEN GRINDING Dip the tool constantly into cold water to keep it cool.

Do not press too hard against the wheel to avoid "burning" the steel.

Grind away from the cutting edge of a tool such as an engraving tool. If you grind towards the cutting edge you are apt to carry the friction heat towards the thin edge and "burn" the steel.

12. WIRE DRAWING AND TUBE FORMING

WIRE DRAWING Wire can be thinned and shaped by means of draw plates. Draw plates are made with different shaped holes:—the round, square, half round, and rectangular ones are popular with metal workers. Note from figure 51 that the holes in the draw plate become progressively smaller. Note too from the cross-sectional diagram (fig. 52) that each hole tapers from the back side of the draw plate almost to the front and then becomes straight for a short distance.

To thin a wire, taper one end of the wire with a rough file, then insert it into the proper hole in the back of the draw plate, and pull it through with the aid of draw tongs.

Occasional annealing (see annealing) will keep a wire soft and thus keep it from breaking. Bee's wax, used as a lubricant, will help the operation and prolong the life of the draw plate. It is best to warm the wire slightly, especially gold, when applying the wax. A draw bench can be employed for drawing very thick wires.

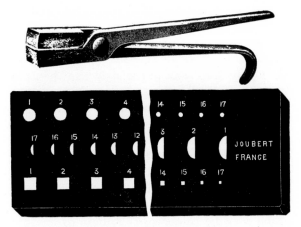

Fig. 51 Draw Tongs and Plate

TUBE FORMING Tubes are formed from flat sheet metal by pulling the sheet through the round holes of a draw plate. The width of the sheet should be 3 times the width of the required tube, and the thickness of the sheet depends upon the desired wall thickness of the tube.

TUBE FORMING PROCEDURE

1. Mark off the required width with a divider along a straight edge of the metal and then cut this piece off with shears. File, if necessary, to make the sides parallel.
2. Point one end of the strip with shears.
3. Start forming the strip into a tube by placing it over a groove in a piece of wood or a swage block and then hammering

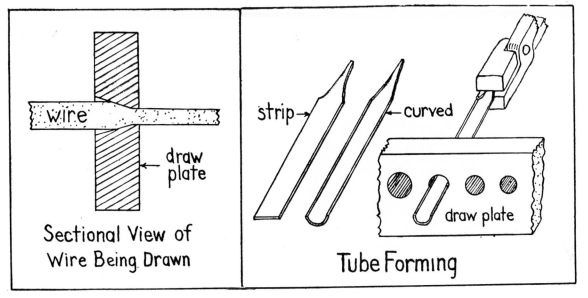

Sectional View of Wire Being Drawn

Tube Forming

Fig. 52   Fig. 53

down on the strip to curve it. Any narrow hammer with round edges or even a rod can be used. Curve the edges as much as possible.

4. Apply bee's wax to the strip and then pull it through the draw plate to form a tube.
5. Just before the strip closes, a knife blade may be held in the opening to straighten the seam.
6. Draw the tube to the required diameter.

The tube may be straightened by annealing and then hammering or rolling on a flat, smooth surface. If desired, the seam of the tube may be soldered. It is best to cut sections off the tube with a jeweler's saw.

If a tube with an accurate inside diameter is required, the tube may be formed and drawn around a steel wire. The wire should be oiled so that it can be removed; to remove the wire, place it through a hole in the draw plate that will hold the tube and then pull it out.

13. DOMES, SPHERES, SPIRALS, SHOT, CONES, AND PYRAMIDS

DOMES Domes are semi-spheres that are best formed in a dapping block (fig. 54) though a lead block may be used. The diameter of the circular disc must be larger than the required dome, approximately 1/3 larger to make a half sphere. Circular discs may be purchased or they may be cut to shape with a shear or saw from a larger piece of metal.

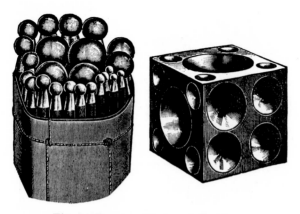

Fig. 54 Dapping Block and Punches

Fig. 55 Three methods of forming a spiral

The gauge of the metal depends on the size and design of the object.

To form a dome, place the metal level in an appropriate hollow in the dapping block and hammer it to shape with steel dapping punches or, better yet, for larger domes, with wooden punches. The tops of many file handles make excellent punches. To make a semi-sphere, keep moving the metal while shaping it from larger to smaller hollows in the block until the required shape is obtained. The sphere may be filed while it is in the dapping block.

If a lead block is used to form the sphere, the hollows are punched into the lead with steel dapping tools. The procedure then is the same as above, only all traces of lead which may adhere to the metal must be removed with emery paper or a glass fiber brush.

A small dome may be formed on part of a flat sheet of metal by placing the metal over the required hollow in the dapping block. A slightly smaller punch than the hollow in the block is hammered down to form the dome in the metal.

SPHERES Spheres are made by soldering together two semi-spheres, made as described above. A tiny hole must be drilled in one to permit air to escape and re-enter during the soldering operation otherwise the sphere may collapse as it cools or explode if re-heated.

SPIRALS A spiral is best formed from round, square or rectangular wire as follows: File one end of the wire on one side only to taper it (fig. 55). The end of the wire may be forged, if desired, to a taper.

Grip the very end of the wire with smooth jawed round nose or half-round chain nose pliers. Hold the wire fairly firm with the pliers and start to bend the wire in. While bending, permit the pliers to slip and snap off the end of the wire. By so doing, the spiral can be curved or started from the very end of the wire.

Now that the spiral has been started, hold the beginning of the spiral firmly with the plier and then bend the wire (or turn the plier) to form the spiral. A pleasingly shaped open spiral (fig. 55 top) can be formed the above way. Note:—the spiral is formed by holding the wire with the pliers at the very tip and no other place.

The tip of the wire for a closed spiral (fig. 55 center) is started the same way as above. After the start, the tip is squeezed together with a plier until it is closed. Now the beginning of the spiral is held sideways between the flat jaws of a flat or snipe nose pliers and it is then bent to form the spiral.

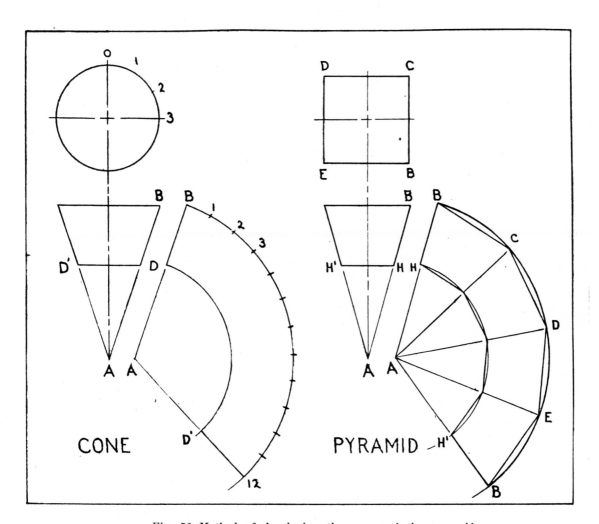

Fig. 56 Method of developing the cone and the pyramid

After the wire has been coiled several times the coil or spiral may be held in one's fingers and the coiling may be continued until the proper sized spiral has been achieved.

A closed spiral can be formed quickly by bending about ½″ of one end of the wire to be spiraled at right angles (fig. 55 bottom). Then grip the bent end of the wire in the

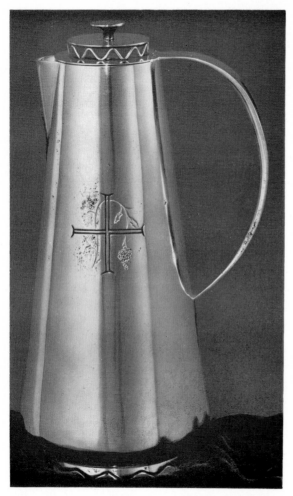

Fig. 57 Wine Flagon   Harold A. Milbrath

side jaws of a parallel-jawed plier. Turn the long end of the wire to form the spiral. Wires 14 gauge or thicker may have to be annealed before the first turn is completed. After the spiral has been formed to the proper size, the bent starting end is nipped off leaving the spiral shown in figure 55 bottom.

SHOT Shot are small, solid balls of metal which have many ornamental uses in silver-smithing, art metal and jewelry work. They are made by melting pure silver, sterling silver, brass, etc., on a charcoal block. Scrap metal may be used to make shot; however, if many shot are required of the same size, it is best to use wire. The wire is wrapped around a rod, in a manner similar to link making, and after it is removed, the coiled wire is cut with a nipper to form rings. The rings when melted will form shot of equal size.

If perfectly round balls are desired, little concave impressions of the proper size are made in the charcoal with a small dapping punch, over which the metal is melted. If the concave impression is not made the balls will be slightly flat on the bottom. Use a sharp flame in order to melt the metal quickly; however, as soon as the balls are formed, change the flame, by using less air, to a soft flame in order to slowly cool the balls; otherwise they are apt to become pitted. The balls should be pickled before they are soldered to the jewelry object.

Excellent silver shot can be made by melting the silver on a piece of wood. The formed shot are unusually smooth, but slightly flat on the bottom. This method is worth trying, especially when charcoal isn't available.

CONES Cones and sections of cones can be made from flat sheet as follows:

On the same center line, the front and top view of the cone is drawn as shown in figure 56. The top is divided into four equal parts and then with a divider one of the parts is divided into three equal parts. Distance 0 to 1 then represents 1/12 of the circumference of the top of the cone. Distance A-B is marked off on the metal, and with a divider and A as center and A-B as radius an arc is drawn. Along the arc, starting from B, 12 lengths, 0 to 1 are then marked off. At the twelfth point a line is drawn back to A thus completing the pattern for the cone.

A section (frustrum) of a cone is developed in the same manner as the completed cone with the line added as shown in the diagram.

After the metal has been cut to the required pattern it is bent to cone shape, if wide, over a blowhorn stake or, if narrow, a beakhorn stake. A "T" stake may be used for a frustrum of a cone.

PYRAMIDS Sections (frustrums) of pyramids can be made from flat sheet in a manner somewhat similar to that used for cones. Figure 56 shows how the front and top view are drawn. Then, on the metal, with A as center, the arcs are drawn and along the arc formed from B, distances B-C, C-D, D-E and E-B are marked off and then connected to A with straight lines. Line H-H' is drawn.

The bending lines of small pyramids are scored with a three corner file and after the metal is bent to shape, solder is applied to each corner to reenforce it. The bending lines of large pyramids are scored with a grooving tool in a manner similar to that described for boxes on page 82.

14. RIVETING, GROOVED SEAM AND TUBE BENDING

RIVETING Aluminum, copper, brass, and iron rivets can be purchased with round, oval, or flat heads with diameters of 1/16 to ¼ inch and lengths from 1/4 to 1 inch.

To rivet two pieces of metal together, first drill holes through them the same size as the rivets. Then place the rivet in position and, if necessary, cut the projecting part of the rivet (the shank) to the proper length — which for a round headed rivet is 1½ times the rivet's thickness. Now the clearance hole in the rivet set is placed over the rivet and the set is hammered to force the two metals together (fig. 58).

The rivet is set and headed as follows:— with a flat face of a ball peen hammer, hammer down on the shank of the rivet to spread it as shown in figure 58. The round head is formed by placing the concaved depression in the rivet set over the spread shank and then hammering the set firmly (fig. 58). If a faceted rivet head is desired, do not use the rivet set; round the spread shank of the rivet with the round head of the ball peen hammer.

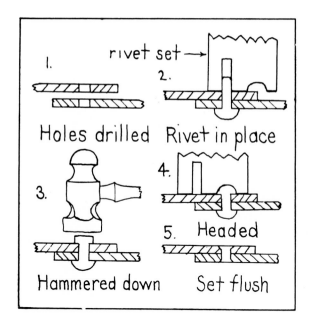

Fig. 58 Riveting

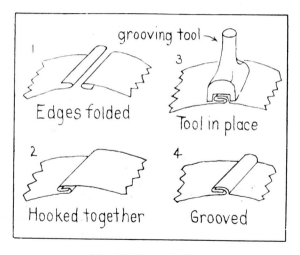

Fig. 59 Grooved Seam

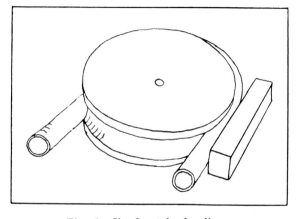

Fig. 60 Jig for tube bending

Fig. 61 Multi-Former bending 3/8" tubing

If both sides of the rivet are to be round, set the rivet by placing the round head of the rivet over the concave in another rivet set. If the rivet is to be flush on one or both sides, countersink the metal on one or both sides and hammer the shank of the rivet to spread it into the countersunk area. If a

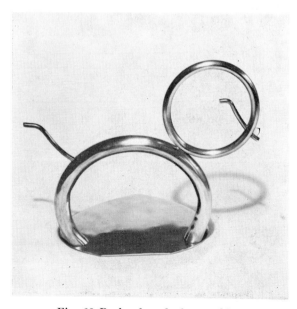

Fig. 62 Bookend made from tubing

number of rivets are to be used, drill the first set of holes and place a rivet in those holes. Then drill the other holes; thus all holes will be aligned.

GROOVED SEAM Thin (22, 24 gauge) flat metal such as copper and brass can quickly, easily, and efficiently be joined by a grooved seam. The seam is made as shown in figure 59. The edges can be bent over 1/16" sheet metal or, in school shops, in a bar folder or brake. The edges then are locked together and placed on a stake. The grooving tool should be hammered down with a mallet. The tool can be purchased with different widths:—1/8" is popular for small art metal objects.

TUBE BENDING The walls of a tube will collapse when being bent unless the tube is first filled with lead or bent in a machine. It usually is best to anneal the tube before bending it.

To fill a tube with lead, first plug one end with wood. Now pour machine oil into the tube in order to coat the inner walls, and then pour the excess out:— this will prevent the lead from adhering. Melt the lead in a ladle and pour it into the tube with a continuous pour. To remove the lead after the tube has been bent, start heating the tube from its ends and work toward the center.

Caution:—When melting lead keep water away for water will cause the molten lead to explode or spatter.

The tubing, with the lead inside, can be bent by hand or around a form. It is best however, to bend the tube in the type of jig shown in figure 60, the center of which was turned in a lathe.

Wood's metal, a low melting alloy of 4 parts lead, 2 parts tin, and 1 part cadmium, is used industrially for bending narrow tubes. Since Wood's metal has a melting point (141° F.) below that of boiling water (212° F.), the metal can easily be melted and removed from a bent tube by immersing the tube in hot water.

Several excellent bending machines (fig. 61) are on the market. The machines have interchangeable parts which can be used for many bending operations. The Multi-Former (fig. 61) is a cleverly designed vise that has three rollers which fit into holes in the top of the vise. The rollers sold with the machine will bend tubes of $\frac{1}{4}$, $\frac{3}{8}$, or $\frac{1}{2}$ inch diameter. To bend a tube, place it between the rollers and tighten the jaws of the vise. Roll the tube back and forth and continue to tighten the jaws until the desired curve in the tube is obtained.

Note:—The extreme ends (about one inch) can not be formed. If a ring is desired, add an additional two inches to the required length, roll the tube to form the ring, cut the ends off, file and silver solder, then roll again to form a perfect ring as shown in the novelty bookends in figure 62.

15. TRANSFERRING DESIGNS

The following method is recommended for transferring to the metal a design which is to be cut to shape with a jeweler's saw or is to be chased.

Trace the design with a sharp, hard (No. 3) pencil onto a piece of tracing paper. Heat the metal slightly to warm it, and while it is still warm rub a piece of yellow bee's wax over it to leave a thin layer. Let the metal cool to room temperature. This can be done quickly by placing the metal on a thick piece of steel which will conduct the heat from it.

Now place the tracing paper on the wax, graphite side down. With a smooth surface, such as a burnishing tool or the handle of some pliers, rub the tracing paper until the wax shows through and then slowly remove the tracing paper. A graphite design should be on the wax.

Scratch the design onto the metal through the wax with a scratch awl, warm the metal again and wipe the wax off with a rag to complete the transfer of the design to the metal. Note: if monograms or letters are transferred, the design must be retraced on the opposite side of the tracing paper for it to appear properly.

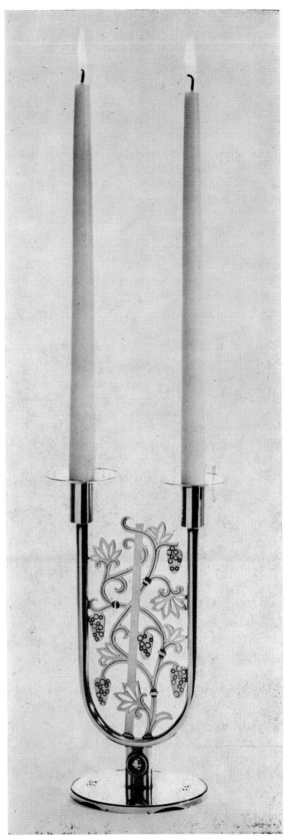

Fig. 63 Sterling Candlestick by Carl Podszus

FORMING TECHNIQUES

Forming or raising of flat or sheet metal into useful and artistic shapes by hand can be separated into the following classifications: namely, Beating Down, Straight Raising, Combination Raising, Angular Raising, Seaming and Assembled Construction. Each classification is thoroughly explained below.

DIAGRAM It is important in all classifications that the shape of the object to be formed be drawn full size on paper. A template (fig. 66-1) is then made from the drawing. The metal is then shaped with the aid of the template exactly to the shape of the drawing. It is poor technique and often a waste of time to form the metal without a definite, carefully worked out plan.

METAL THICKNESS The metal thickness generally used for raising sheet copper, brass and silver by hand is 18 gauge (.040). 20 gauge silver is often used since it is less expensive, and so is 20 gauge copper used when weight is a factor. Thicker gauges (14 and 16) of aluminum and pewter are popular.

1. BEATING DOWN

The beating down method is by far the easiest and quickest way of hand forming silver, copper, and other metals into useful objects. The method is especially adaptable for forming bowls and the making of the shallow bowl, figure 64, will be used to illustrate the method. The required tools are shown in figure 65.

Note: The size of the hollow in the wood forming block (fig. 66-2) does not predetermine the size of the finished bowl. The hollow in the block (3″ wide and 1″ deep) permits the metal to give under the weight of the hammer blow. Almost any sized bowl can be formed in the same block.

Fig. 64 Bowl with ring base

REQUIRED METAL The diameter of the required metal disc to form the shallow bowl is easily obtained from the front view of the drawing (fig. 66-1). The distance A—B is the required radius (twice this distance is the diameter). With a divider (or compass) set to the above radius, a circle is drawn onto the metal which is then cut to shape as explained in figure 33A.

STARTING PROCEDURE To form the bowl, place the metal as shown in figure 66-3. The metal is raised approximately 20 degrees. With a silversmith hammer, firmly hit the metal directly down starting about ½ inch in from the edge. Since the metal is over the hollow in the block, it will give under the hammer blow. Rotate the metal and continue the hammering until the starting position has been reached.

Note: The wrinkles that have been formed. Be careful that they do not become so deep that they fold over and eventually produce a crack in the metal. The wrinkles are removed as they appear by hammering straight down upon them.

To deepen the bowl, continue the hammering process, this time, however, striking the metal about an inch in from the other blows. When the starting point has been reached again, shift the hammer blows in towards the center—and continue the process until the center of the bowl is reached.

The bowl, if desired, can be deepened by repeating the above process from the beginning again. The second time, however, hold the metal at a steeper (45°) angle over the hollow in the forming block.

ANNEALING The hammering in the forming process stretches and hardens the metal, so much so that the metal becomes difficult to shape and also may crack. Annealing (see page 28) will soften the metal so that it may be worked easily again. Most shallow bowls can be formed without annealing.

CHECKING The shape of the bowl is best checked by means of the template (fig. 66-1) which will show quickly where the metal must be hammered to match the original working or mechanical drawing. The bowl's curvature can also be checked by observing it when held arms length at eye level or by holding it edge down against the front view of the mechanical drawing.

TRUING After the metal has been formed to the proper shape, the bumps left by the silversmith hammer are removed by striking the metal over a domed stake with a flat-faced mallet. The curvature of the stake should be slightly less than that of the inside curvature of the bowl (fig. 66-8). Strike the metal vigorously with the mallet to remove the bumps. It is best to strike the metal over the same position of the stake and to move the metal to different positions. In other words, move the metal and not the mallet. Start from the center of the bowl and work out to its edge in all directions.

PLANISHING The metal is planished primarily to make it hard and smooth. The planishing hammer, if used properly, leaves a pleasant, faceted hammer mark on the metal. In Colonial American days, silversmiths removed the planishing mark by polishing. Today, many craftsmen, not all, feel that the planishing mark is a true indication of a handmade object. The bowl is planished on the same stake that was used for truing. The preferred planishing hammer is the one (8 ounce) shown in figure 65. It is best, especially for beginners, to draw concentric circles on the bowl with a pencil compass (about ½″ apart, as guide lines).

The bowl is held over the stake as shown in figure 66-9. The planishing is started in the exact center of the bowl. When the center has been completed, the planishing operation is continued away from the center the width of the hammer mark. The planishing operation is now continued in a circular direction using the concentric circles as guides. The process is continued and each time as one circle of planishing marks is completed the metal is shifted for the next row of marks, and so on until the edge of the bowl is reached. It is best to change the direction of rotation of the metal after each circle of hammer blows is completed in order to eliminate any twisting effect.

Note: The planishing hammer strikes the stake in approximately the same position during the entire operation. In other words, the metal is moved, not the hammer. This way the planishing blow can be similar and the contour of the metal can be controlled better since the shape of the stake remains the same.

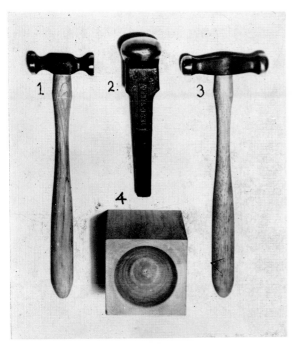

Fig. 65 Required tools 1. Planishing hammer 2. Domed stake 3. Forming hammer 4. Forming block

BOWL FORMING PROCEDURE

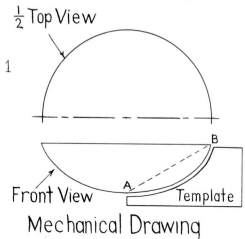

1 ½ Top View

Front View   Template

A   B

Mechanical Drawing

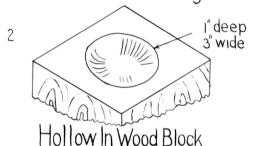

2   1" deep
    3" wide

Hollow In Wood Block

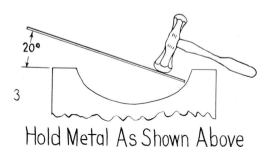

20°

3

Hold Metal As Shown Above

4

Start (½ in) From Edge-Work In
Circular Fashion In Towards Center

5

Hammer Center Straight Down

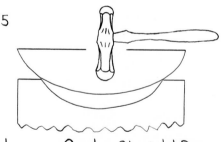

6

Shallow Bowl Formed Without Annealing

7

Deeper Bowl Requires Annealing

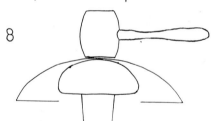

8

Smooth With Mallet

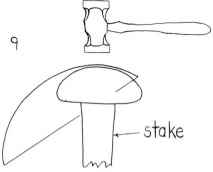

9   stake

Planish:-Start From Center
Work In Circular Fashion
To Edge

MB

Fig. 67 Planishing the bowl

The planishing hammer is lifted no more than 2 or 3 inches above the metal and then the metal is struck with a firm blow. Strike the metal with the center of the face of the hammer (fig. 67). Avoid turning the hammer so that its edge hits the metal and leaves an objectionable mark.

The force required to work the hammer is obtained from the wrist. Never use the planishing hammer as you would a nail or claw hammer which obtains its power from the elbow. By using the wrist, a rapid continuous blow can be maintained for long periods without too much exertion.

CHECKING AGAIN When the bowl has been completely planished, its shape is then checked again by means of the template. If high or low spots are observed, they can be treated as follows:—

Low Areas By planishing the low areas again, the low areas will rise for planishing stretches the metal. The low areas and the metal can only go up if it is struck with the hammer directly above the stake. **Caution:** do not hammer only in one spot for then the metal will bulge out only in that spot. Hammer on the spot and around it until the metal is raised to the desired height.

High Areas may be lowered by hammering the metal with a planishing hammer lightly over the stake or by holding the metal so the high spot just does not touch the stake. This way the metal can be lowered to the proper height.

FINISHING THE BOWL The outer edge of the bowl may be filed flat and left plain or it may be fluted, crimped, scalloped, pierced, or treated as desired.

The base of the bowl in figure 64 was made by bending and hard soldering a strip of 18 gauge metal to form a ring. After soldering, the ring was planished, filed until it matched the bottom of the bowl and then it was soft soldered in position.

FORMED BASE FOR BOWL A base can be formed directly on the bowl by using the technique shown in figure 68. First the desired base circle is scribed on the bowl with a divider. Then the center of the bowl is hammered down. This is best done by starting in the center and then by moving the hammer blow out gradually to the scribed base circle (fig. 68-2).

A rod of a hard wood such as maple is placed in a vise. A cut off section of an old baseball bat can be used. The bowl is held firmly down over the rod as shown in figure 68-4. By hammering the bottom edge straight

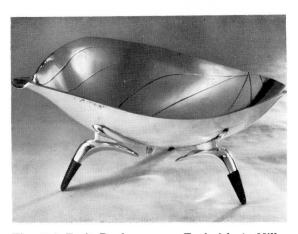

Fig. 67A Fruit Bowl   Frederick A. Miller

down in the position shown in figure 68-4 and by moving the bowl (not the hammer) slowly along the base circle, a sharp edge can be formed. This edge can be sharpened by hammering the side edge as shown in figure 68-5. The center of the bowl is finally replanished as shown in figure 68-6.

STRETCHING METHOD If a very thick edge is desired on a bowl, the so-called stretching method can be used. In this method, employed by several contemporary craftsmen, one starts with a thick piece of metal, as thick as eight gauge or as thick as the edge desired. The metal object is thinned and formed away from its edge towards its center, working in a circle, with a heavy forming hammer. Hammer the metal over a smooth flat piece of steel or over an anvil. The final form of the bowl is obtained as explained in the beating down method. Deeper objects in the stretching method can be obtained by employing other techniques described in this book.

Note: the metal must be annealed often. The edge can be further thickened by hammering directly down upon it before each annealing with a collet or planishing hammer. The fruit bowl by Frederick A. Miller (fig. 67A) was made by the stretching method.

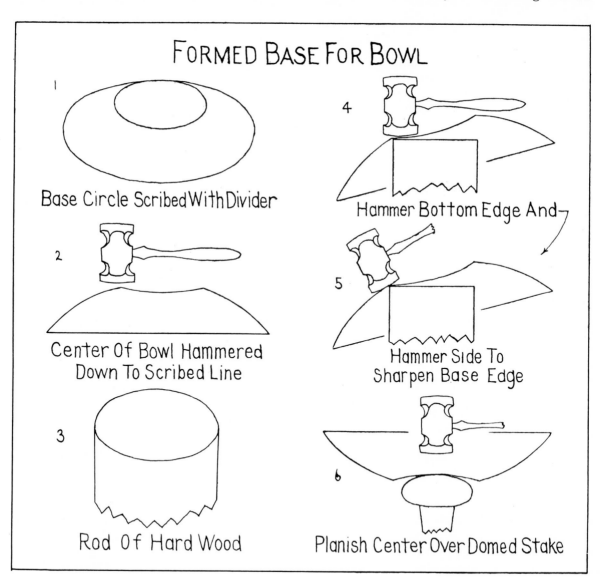

FORMED BASE FOR BOWL

1. Base Circle Scribed With Divider

2. Center Of Bowl Hammered Down To Scribed Line

3. Rod Of Hard Wood

4. Hammer Bottom Edge And

5. Hammer Side To Sharpen Base Edge

6. Planish Center Over Domed Stake

Fig. 68

2. STRAIGHT RAISING

Objects with flat bases and straight sides that can not be made by the beating down process can be formed by the straight raising method. The tray shown in figure 69 will be used to explain the method. As stated previously, the diagram should be drawn carefully and then a template (fig. 71-1) is made from it.

REQUIRED METAL. The diameter of the disc required to make the tray can be determined directly from the full sized diagram (fig. 71-1) by adding its greatest width (W) to its greatest height (H). This measurement (the diameter) is then divided by two to get the proper radius. The circle is scribed onto the metal with a divider and then is cut to shape with a shear.

STARTING PROCEDURE The base circle, where the raising is to start, is scribed into the disc with a divider. The metal disc is then held at a 45° angle against the raising stake (fig. 72) with the scribed line of the base circle against the edge of the stake. The long or short wood stake (fig. 70) or a steel stake can be used. The raising hammer strikes the metal at the angle shown in figure 72. The hammer blow should be light for its purpose is merely to locate the edge where the metal is to be raised. The metal is rotated after each blow until the entire base edge, 1/4″ high, has been formed as shown in figure 71-2.

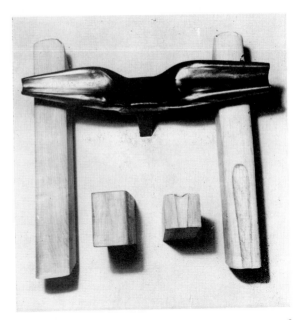

Fig. 70 Long and short wood raising stakes, wood crimping stakes, steel crimping stake.

CRIMPING By means of crimping, the metal disc can be raised quickly and the shape of the finished object can be controlled accurately. **Note:** the metal can be raised without crimping; however, it is better to crimp —more on the subject later.

Proceed as follows: Divide the metal disc with pencil lines into 12 sections (fig. 71-3). Note the crimping block and type of hammer that can be used (fig. 72A). Hammer the metal slightly near the base circle and deepen the crimp near the circumference of the disc. Crimp the metal in the order shown by the numbers in figure 71-3 in order to avoid distorting the metal. The raised base edge that was formed before the crimping prevents the crimping from going into the base of the metal. After crimping, the metal should look like that in figure 71-5.

RAISING CONTINUED Continue the raising process over the wood stake. Hold the metal at the angle shown in figure 73 and hammer the metal lightly at first. Raise only 1/2″ of metal height at a time and rotate the metal after each blow. When, after each rotation of the metal, the starting point has been reached, raise another 1/2″ of metal; and so on until the edge of the metal has been reached.

Fig. 69 Tray formed by straight raising

STRAIGHT RAISING PROCEDURE

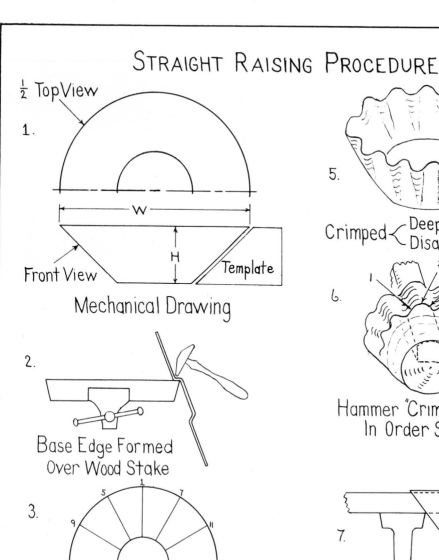

1. ½ TopView

W

H

Front View   Template

Mechanical Drawing

2. Base Edge Formed Over Wood Stake

3. Disc Divided For Crimping

4. Crimping Block and Stake

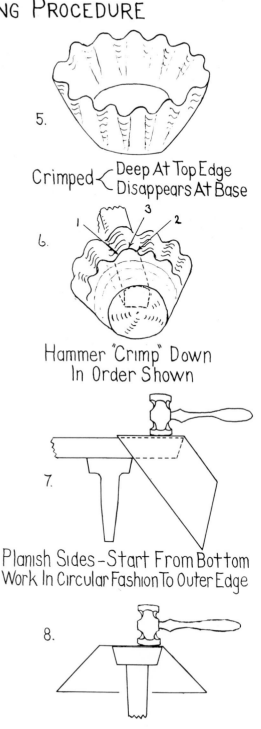

5. Crimped ⟨ Deep At Top Edge / Disappears At Base

6. Hammer "Crimp" Down In Order Shown

7. Planish Sides – Start From Bottom Work In Circular Fashion To Outer Edge

8. Planish Bottom – Start At Edge Work In Circular Fashion To Center

Fig. 71

Note: the hammer blow must be directed as shown in figure 71-6. The blows are placed from the sides of each individual crimp towards the center of the crimp (blows 1 and 2). The center of the crimp is hammered last (blow 3) for if hammered first the metal may fold over upon itself and this would eventually result in a hole in the object. Heavy hammer blows will be required to force the metal together as one approaches the edge; at the very edge, however, use a lighter blow to avoid stretching the edge.

BOUGING The object is now bouged:—that is, hammered with a slightly domed planishing hammer inorder to smooth the rough surface bumps left by raising. Use a steel stake, the type shown in figure 1-9, and a medium weight (12 ounce) planishing hammer. Hold the metal object directly on the stake as shown in figure 71-7. First hammer the bottom edge of the metal lightly. Rotate the metal after each blow the width of the hammer mark and continue hammering until the starting point has been reached. Then raise the hammer the height of the hammer blow and with a firmer blow continue the process:—and so on until the edge of the metal is reached.

Note: this process is a rough one; its purpose is mainly to smooth very rough spots. It is best to rotate the metal in the opposite direction after each circle of blows has been completed; this keeps the object from becoming twisted. After the bottom edge has been hammered, pull the metal away from the edge of the stake slightly to avoid cutting the inside bottom edge of the tray.

RAISING COMPLETED Anneal the metal. Again hammer the bottom edge of the metal lightly all around on the wood stake. Then crimp again. Now raise the metal ½″ at a time, working in circles as described previously, until the edge is reached. If done properly, the metal now should be raised to the shape of the tray in figure 69 and should match the template. If necessary, repeat the process until the desired shape is reached; the metal is then ready to be planished.

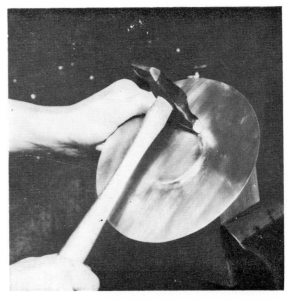

Fig. 72 Forming base edge on wood stake

PLANISHING THE SIDES The sides of the tray are planished over the same type of stake that was used for the bouging operation above. When starting, press the metal firmly against the stake. Use an 8 ounce planishing hammer. Hammer the bottom edge of the tray lightly and carefully so that the edge of the stake will not cut into the inside bottom edge of the tray. **Remember:** rotate the metal and not the hammer when planishing (see page 51). The hammer strikes the stake in the same position. Continue hammering, rotating the metal the width of

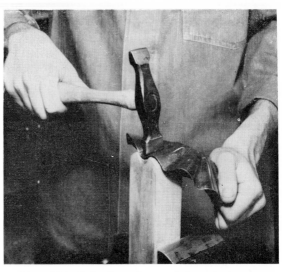

Fig. 72A Crimping the straight raised tray

the hammer mark after each blow, until the starting point has been reached. Then raise the hammer the height of the hammer blow and continue the process:—and so on until the edge of the metal is reached.

Note: Rotate the metal in the opposite direction after completing each row of blows to avoid a twisting effect. Hammer the top edge of the tray a little lighter to avoid thinning it excessively. **Reminder:**—the force required to work the planishing hammer is obtained from the wrist and not from the elbow.

PLANISHING THE BOTTOM The bottom of the tray is planished on the type of flat stake shown in figure 71-8 and with the same flat faced planishing hammer used for planishing the sides of the tray. Start from the bottom edge of the tray and with the aid of concentric pencil circles planish to the center of the tray.

Note: The edge of the bottom and the bottom edge of the side must be planished very carefully. Often after the bottom edge has been planished it is necessary to replanish parts of the side edge very lightly. This is best done over the same flat stake used for the bottom planishing. The metal object is held firmly down against the stake and the side edge is then planished where necessary.

Fig. 74 Beaker   Paul Revere, 1795
Courtesy of the Metropolitan Museum of Art

Note: Only the center of the planishing hammer hits the metal:—see figure 77-3 for position of the hammer. By planishing the bottom and the side edge carefully a perfectly rounded bottom can be made.

SETTING THE BOTTOM The planishing operation will harden the bottom metal and also stretch it so that it will become convexed or raised slightly. Thus the tray when placed on a table will not rest properly and will rock. The bottom should be slightly concave so that the tray rests only on its edge. This is done by placing the tray bottom up on a bench and by hammering the bottom with a flat planishing hammer. Start from the outer edge and, working in circles, work in towards the center. Hammer lightly to avoid denting the metal. Not many blows are required to change the shape of the bottom from the convex (raised) to the slightly concave (lowered) shape.

Now place the tray bottom down on a smooth wood or steel surface (a surface plate is ideal) and check to see if the tray rests firmly. It it rocks, the rocking can be corrected by one or a combination of both of the following methods:

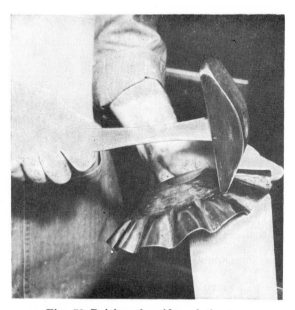

Fig. 73 Raising the sides of the tray

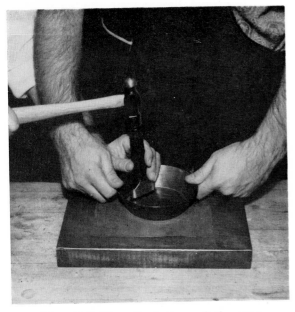

Fig. 75 Setting the bottom of the tray

Method 1: Rub the tray back and forth on a surface plate or some other smooth surface. This will indicate several of the high spots. Turn the tray over and tap the spots down with a planishing hammer. Try again for rocking, repeat the hammering, if necessary, until the tray does not rock.

Method 2: Place the tray on a surface plate or other smooth surface. Place several sheets of newspaper or, if available, a piece of thin leather between the tray and the surface plate. Have a helper hold the tray on opposite sides so that it can be pressed firmly down against the surface plate. Then place a wood or steel setting or tracing stake (fig. 75) against the inner edge of the tray. Now hammer the stake and while hammering move the stake so that it presses against the inner edge of the tray. Hammer where required. Check the tray and if necessary repeat until the tray rests firmly without rocking. Why the paper or leather between the tray and the surface plate? The paper or leather permits the metal to give slightly when the setting stake is hammered.

FINISHING THE TRAY The top edge of the tray may be filed flat and left plain or it may be fluted, crimped, scalloped, etc.

In whatever type of edge used, it is best to level and, if necessary, trim the top first. Blocks of wood (fig. 76) may be used for leveling purposes. The leveling is done by holding the point of a pencil or a scriber on a block of wood against the lowest height of the edge of the tray. Now spin the tray slowly in order to scratch a line completely around the tray. File the tray to this line or, if necessary, trim the edge to the line. The trimming is done with a small (7") curved shear. Hold the shear and cut the metal as shown in figure 34. Now planish the edge of the tray lightly to remove any small wrinkles that may have developed while cutting the metal. Finally the edge of the tray is filed to complete the tray.

TECHNICAL INFORMATION The outer edge of raised objects becomes thicker—the metal is pushed together. The edge of high raised objects may be thickened to twice its original thickness by careful raising. If a thicker edge is desired, it can be had by hammering down (colleting) on the outer edge of the metal with a colleting or domed planishing hammer after each annealing.

NARROW EDGES The raising of a narrow edge is a variation of straight raising that can be used to form such items as coasters

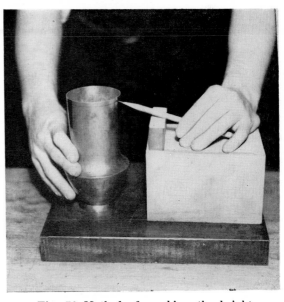

Fig. 76 Method of marking the height

and low bases for bowls. The techniques for making the coaster in figure 77 is as follows:

Planish the top side of a 3″ diameter—18 gauge disc and then anneal. With a divider, scribe a 2½″ diameter circle on the back side of the disc. Place the disc, back side up, over a steel bottom stake, steel rod, or even over a cut-off section of a baseball bat. The diameter of the bottom stake or rod should be slightly smaller than the diameter of the required coaster.

With a planishing hammer, tap the edge of the disc down slightly as shown in figure 77-3. Continue hammering the edge down while rotating the disc until the edge is raised as desired. Now the coaster is planished as explained in the preceeding chapter on straight raising.

NOTE: If a seamless base for a bowl is desired after the edge has been raised, cut out the metal inside the scribed circle with a jeweler's saw and then planish the edge or base metal over a raising stake.

The edge of the coaster can be left plain or treated as shown in figure 77-5. The center of the tray can be chased or etched.

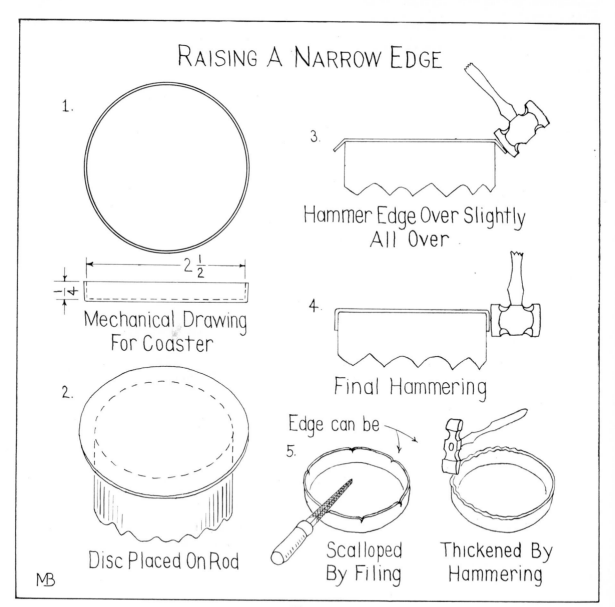

RAISING A NARROW EDGE

1.

$2\frac{1}{2}$

Mechanical Drawing For Coaster

2. Disc Placed On Rod

3. Hammer Edge Over Slightly All Over

4. Final Hammering

5. Edge can be —

Scalloped By Filing

Thickened By Hammering

Fig. 77

3. COMBINATION RAISING

Punch bowls and other deep bowls are accurately and quickly made by hand by the combination raising method. This method consists of a combination of the raising and the previously described beating down method. The bowl shown in figure 78 will be used to explain the method.

DIAGRAM The diagram or design (fig. 79-1) is drawn full size on paper. On the diagram, or tracing paper if the original diagram is to be kept, the construction lines are plotted. A little judgment is required to plot the lines.

REQUIRED METAL The diameter of the disc required to make the bowl can be determined directly from the full sized diagram, the same method that was used for the straight raised tray. Here too add the greatest width of the object (G-H) to the greatest height (A-Y). This measurement is then divided by two to get the radius of the required disc. The radius is scribed onto the metal with the aid of a divider and the resulting circle is cut to shape with a shear.

STARTING PROCEDURE With a pencil compass and "B" as the center point and "B-D" (taken from the diagram) as a radius, draw a circle onto the metal. The circle is the starting point for raising the metal. Raise

Fig. 78 Bowl—Combination Raising Method

Fig. 80 Silver Bowl   Will Harrison

the metal from this circle to form the side "D-X". Briefly, the raising procedure is as follows:

1. On a wood stake and with a raising hammer, raise the metal only about ½" completely around the pencil circle to form the base edge.
2. Divide the metal disc into 12 sections and crimp.
3. Raise the metal as much as possible.
4. Bouge the metal with a planishing hammer to eliminate rough surface bumps.
5. Anneal, pickle, and then repeat the above until the metal is raised so that the side forms a straight line (D-X). The angle of the side can be checked by holding the metal object, edge down, directly over the full-sized diagram.
6. Anneal and then pickle the metal.

RAISING CONTINUED With a pencil compass, draw a circle to mark the next position (E-F) where the metal is to be raised. Then, from the pencil line, raise the metal (fig. 79-4) to the shape shown in figure 79-5. Again bouge, anneal and pickle the metal.

FINAL SHAPING The final shaping of the object can easily be done by means of the beating down method described previously. First, the bottom of the bowl is hammered down by means of a silversmith hammer over a hollow in a block of wood (fig. 79-6). Start from the edge "D" and work in circular fashion to the center. After the bottom has been shaped, the sides of the bowl are hammered similarly. This time start from the edge "D' and work out in a circular fashion until the outer edge is reached.

CHECKING The final shape of the object is checked with the template which was made from the original diagram. Adjustments, if necessary, are made where required.

BOUGING AND PLANISHING Bouge the object to smooth rough spots. Anneal and pickle. Then it is planished to completely smooth and to harden the metal. In both cases (bouging and planishing) start from the center of the bowl and work, following concentric circle pencil guide lines, out to the edge.

The shape of the required stakes for bouging and planishing depends upon the diameter and shape of the bowl. The curvature of the stakes should match the curvature of the bowl as closely as possible. The bottom of the bowl may be bouged and planished on a domed stake (fig. 65) and the sides may

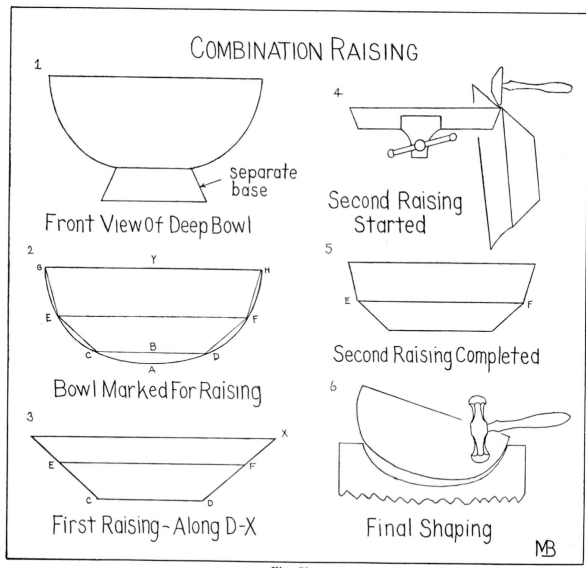

COMBINATION RAISING

1 Front View Of Deep Bowl

separate base

2 Bowl Marked For Raising

3 First Raising ~ Along D-X

4 Second Raising Started

5 Second Raising Completed

6 Final Shaping

Fig. 79

be bouged and planished on a raising or "T" stake (fig. 1-3).

FINISHING The bowl in the illustrated example was finished by straight raising the base shown. After the metal was raised, the bottom was cut out with a jeweler's saw. The edge of the bottom was filed to match the curvature of the bowl and then it was soft soldered to the bowl.

4. ANGULAR RAISING

The cream pitcher shown in figure 81 can best be made by hand from one piece of metal by the angular method. The object, as in the previous methods, must be drawn accurately on paper (fig. 81-1) and a template, for checking purposes, then should be made from the diagram.

REQUIRED METAL The diameter of the disc required to make the pitcher can be determined as described previously, by adding the greatest height (H) to the greatest width (W) and this sum (H + W) will give the diameter of the required disc.

The diameter of the disc can also be determined from figure 81-1 as follows:—add the distances A-B, B-C, C-D, together. This distance is then increased by 2/5. This is then added to the base A-E and the sum will equal the diameter of the disc required to raise the pitcher.

STARTING PROCEDURE The starting procedure for angular raising is similar to that of combination raising. The base circle is scribed onto the metal and starting from the edge A of the base circle, the metal is raised until the side matches line A-B' (fig. 81-2). Bouge, anneal, and pickle the metal. Planish the object from the edge of the base A up to B.

RAISING CONTINUED From B raise the metal so that the side matches B-C' (fig. 81-3). Bouge from B out to the edge. Anneal and then pickle. Planish from B to C. Anneal and pickle again. Now, by means of the

Fig. 82 Angular raised tobacco bowl

Fig. 82A Pitcher formed by angular raising

Fig. 83 Silver teapot   Josiah Austin, 1760
Courtesy of the Metropolitan Museum of Art

63

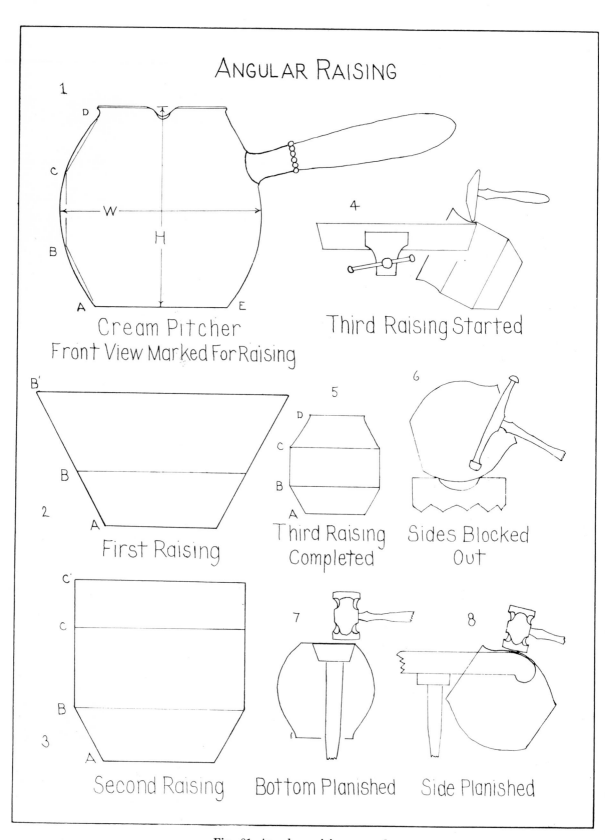

ANGULAR RAISING

1 Cream Pitcher
Front View Marked For Raising

4 Third Raising Started

2 First Raising

5 Third Raising Completed

6 Sides Blocked Out

3 Second Raising

7 Bottom Planished

8 Side Planished

Fig. 81 Angular raising procedure

64

beating down method, hammer out the sides of the object between A-B and B-C so that the metal matches the shape of the diagram. This is best done, since little shaping is required, with a forming or bellying hammer over a slight hollow in a block of wood, over a sand bag, or even by holding the object, if small, in the palm of one's hand and hammering lightly.

NECKING-IN From C the metal is now necked-in so that it matches C-D. The procedure is the same as above; however, it is not necessary to crimp the metal. The object is held as shown in figure 81-4 and the metal is hammered in as if it were being raised. **Note:**—Raising metal without crimping is known as coursing. Be very careful when necking-in that the metal does not overlap and eventually form a crack.

When the metal matches C-D, it is bouged, annealed, pickled, and then planished (fig. 81-8). The top edge is trimmed, hammered out slightly over a stake, and then it is filed.

Check the object with a template or hold it over the diagram to check. Its width also can be checked with a caliper. Make, if required, any necessary changes. Planish and set the bottom as described in method A for the straight raised tray.

The handle can be turned from a piece of ebony or black plastic. It was fitted into the holder soldered to the pitcher. The small spout was hammered out over a piece of wood.

5. SEAMING

This method is recommended for quickly forming by hand high raised objects that would require many hours of tedious labor to form by other hand methods. The pitcher in figure 84 is an example of an object that can be made by the seaming method. The one disadvantage to the method is that the seam that is silver soldered together appears as a light white line on copper or as a thin dark line on silver. The tremendous saving in time, however, more than offsets this slight disadvantage. Often other construction parts such as handles or spouts can be soldered over the soldered seam so that it is

Fig. 84 Seamed silver water pitcher

Fig. 86 Necked-in flower vase

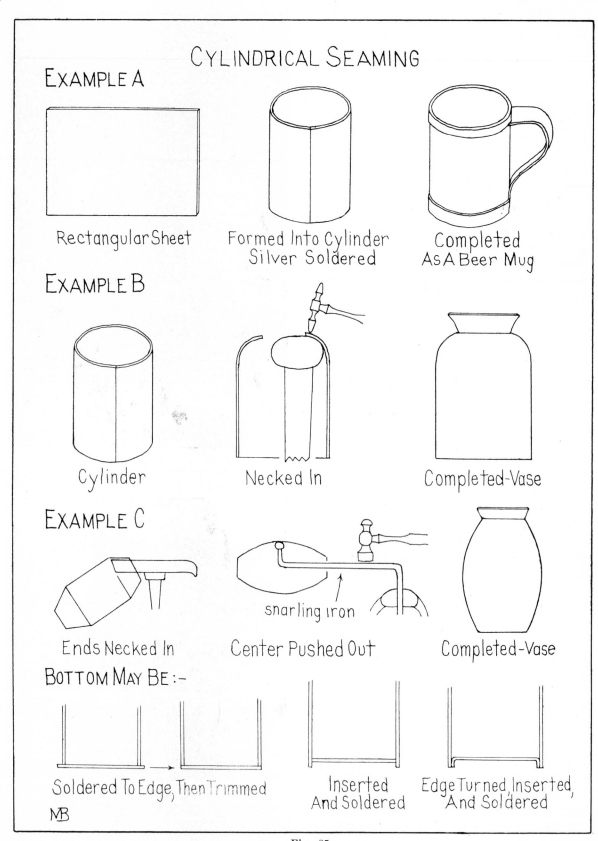

CYLINDRICAL SEAMING

EXAMPLE A

Rectangular Sheet

Formed Into Cylinder
Silver Soldered

Completed
As A Beer Mug

EXAMPLE B

Cylinder

Necked In

Completed-Vase

EXAMPLE C

Ends Necked In

snarling iron

Center Pushed Out

Completed-Vase

BOTTOM MAY BE:-

Soldered To Edge, Then Trimmed

Inserted
And Soldered

Edge Turned, Inserted,
And Soldered

MB

Fig. 85

hidden. Furthermore, if the soldered line is considered undesirable (it really isn't) it can be completely hidden by electro-plating the object when it is completed.

Seaming, for explanation purposes, can be subdivided into the following classifications: namely, cylindrical, tapered, combination, and assembled.

CYLINDRICAL OBJECTS Three methods of shaping cylindrical objects are shown in figure 85.

Example "A" In example "A", the shape of the cylinder is not changed and it is converted into a mug. The making of the mug as an elementary school project is explained on page 117.

The length of the metal required to form a cylinder is found by multiplying the cylinder's diameter by 22/7 or 3.14. The metal, after being cut to size, is bent to form a cylinder over a "T" stake or in a school shop, over a beakhorn stake, or in a slip roll forming machine. **Note:** The object does not have to be perfectly round at this stage; however, it is important that the edges should be filed to form a perfect seam for soldering purposes.

The two edges are held together with binding wire (see figure 21), silver soldered, and then pickled. When planishing, start from one end of the cylinder and hammer around the cylinder, moving the metal, not the hammer, the distance of the planishing mark after each blow. After the first circle of planishing marks has been completed, move the hammer up along the cylinder the width of the hammer mark and planish around the cylinder again. Repeat the above until the entire cylinder is planished. **Note:** The outer edges should be planished a little lighter than the center in order to avoid any overstretching. The planishing will make the metal hard, smooth, and almost into a perfect cylinder so that it can be completed as desired.

Example "B" In example "B", figure 85, one end of the cylinder is necked-in and formed into a vase (fig. 86). The necking-in is done as explained in the chapter on an-

Fig. 87 Necking-in over a domed stake

gular raising. The necking-in of a small object can be done over a domed stake as shown in figure 87. It is best not to attempt to neck-in the entire distance in one hammering for the metal near the edge may

Fig. 88 Necked-in and bellied-out vase

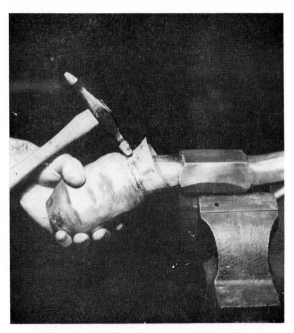

Fig. 89 Necking-in over a "T" stake

overlap. Anneal the metal two or three times. The necked-in cylinder is planished as explained in example "A"; however, the domed stake should be used for the necked-in part of the cylinder.

The top of the flower vase (fig. 86) was developed (fig. 56) silver soldered, planished, and then soft soldered to the necked-in cylinder.

Fig. 90 Bellying-out with a snarling iron

Example "C" In example "C", figure 85, the cylinder was necked-in at both ends and bellied-out in the center to form a vase (fig. 88).

The size of the required metal is determined from the diagram and its construction lines (fig. 85C). Judgment must be employed in planning the construction lines. **Note:** It is easier to neck-in the metal than it is to belly-out; therefore, plan the construction lines accordingly.

After the metal is cut to shape, formed into a cylinder, and then silver soldered, guide lines are drawn with a pencil around the cylinder where the metal is to be necked-in. Both ends of the cylinder are necked-in. The necking-in can be done over a domed stake or over a "T" stake as shown in figure 89.

The center portion is now bellied out by means of the snarling iron as follows: The snarling iron (fig. 85-C) is placed in a vise as shown in figure 90 and the object, where it is to be bellied-out, is pressed down firmly upon the snarling iron. Hammer the iron where shown (about 3″ from the vise) in figure 90. The blow will bend the snarling iron and it will then spring or snap up again, thus pushing the metal out where the metal is pressed against it. Rotate the metal after each blow and continue to rotate the metal until the starting point has been reached. Then move the metal to a new position and repeat the process; and so on until the required shape is obtained. The object to be bellied-out can be held with two hands and a helper can do the hammering.

Note: Just as the necking-in and raising operation require several annealing and hammer operations before the final shape is obtained, bellying the metal also requires several annealing and hammer operations in order to obtain the final shape. It is best to belly-out the center portion of the object after each time the metal is necked-in at the ends so that fewer annealings will be required.

Remember: Work from a template and check the shape of the object with it often. When the desired shape has been obtained, the center of the object may be planished over anvil heads held in an extension iron (fig. 92); the ends of the vase may be planished over a "T" stake.

The bottom of the vase is made as described in the next few paragraphs. The top rim is developed (see figure 56) silver soldered, planished, and soft soldered to the top edge. However, it may be formed from the body of the vase by using a longer piece of metal.

ADDING THE BOTTOM A bottom may be added to the cylinder in one of the following ways (fig. 85):—

By inserting: A disc is cut, planished, filed and then inserted (1/16″ up will do) into the cylinder.

The disc may be soft soldered to the bottom as follows:— apply soft soldered flux, place the solder (three or four small pieces will do) along the edge, and apply heat mainly to the outer edge of the cylinder until the solder runs neatly around the seam. If the center of the disc is heated only, the solder, since it runs to the hottest part of the metal, may run away from the edge towards the center of the disc.

The disc may be hard soldered to the cylinder; however, the required heat would soften the metal so that it would have to be replanished. Use hard solder for sterling silver objects or where great strength is required. If hard solder is used, tie the cylinder with binding wire so that the original seam will not open. Apply flux. Cut or stick solder can be used. It is best to turn the cylinder on its side so that the bottom will not drop out, and to roll the cylinder as the solder melts and flows.

Narrow Edge: A narrow edge (1/8″) may be formed on the disc by hammering (see fig. 77) or in school shops where a sheet metal burring machine is available the edge can be formed by turning or burring. After the edge has been formed, the center of the disc is planished. The disc is then inserted into the cylinder, formed edge out, and is then soft soldered. After soldering, the bottom is filed flat.

Fig. 91 Vase—necked-in and bellied-out

To The Outer Edge Cut the disc for the bottom a little larger (1/8″ will do) than the base of the cylinder and then planish. File the base of the cylinder perfectly flat and then place it on the disc. Now the disc can be silver soldered to the cylinder and after it has been soldered it can be trimmed with the 7″ curved plate shears and filed to match the cylinder.

Fig. 92 Extension arm with different anvil heads

TAPERED OBJECTS

Round tapered objects are sections (frustrums) of cones. They are formed or developed as explained in figure 56. The coffee pot in figure 178 and the flower vase in figure 93 are objects that have been designed with straight tapered sides.

A method for holding binding wire on a tapered object is shown in figure 93A. Note that several wires are looped in two positions and then placed through the tapered object. Wire is now placed through the loops and then tightened to hold the edges to be

Fig. 93A Tapered object bound for soldering

as shown in figure 22. If necessary, a large poker can be used to align the edges while they are being silver soldered.

The teapot in figure 94 was constructed from the frustrum of a cone. The bottom end was necked-in over a domed stake. The base was straight raised from a disc. It was inserted into and silver soldered to the bottom. The cover knob also was constructed from the frustrum of a cone.

Fig. 93 Tapered flower vase

soldered firmly together. If the looped wire isn't used, the binding wire slips down the tapered sides of the object and thus remains loose. The soldering is done as shown in figure 22.

Experienced craftsmen often solder tapered objects without binding wire. This is done by filing the edges to form a perfect seam. The edges are bent past one another so that the metal develops spring which will hold the edges together when they are snapped back into position. The metal is placed

Fig. 94 Teapot—tapered and necked-in construction

COMBINATION SEAMED AND
RAISED CONSTRUCTION

The urn shown in figure 95 was made by the combination seamed and raised construction technique. The top of the vase was formed by seaming. This fits into a bowl shaped section that was formed by angular raising. The concaved collar was formed from a ring as shown in figure 95A. The base was made from one piece of metal in a similar

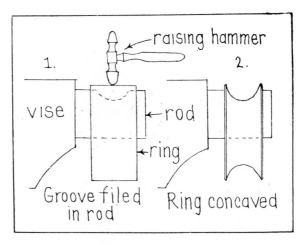

Fig. 95A Method of forming a concaved collar

6. ASSEMBLED CONSTRUCTION

The objects in figures 97, 98, and 99 are examples of assembled construction. The silver cream pitcher (fig. 97) was assembled (constructed) by first bending the body metal to the desired shape. Then the back and finally the bottom and handle were soldered in position to complete the object. The back and bottom metal were cut slightly larger than required and filed to the proper curvature after soldering.

The sides and bottom of the teapot in

Fig. 95 Urn—Combination construction

fashion to the method used to form a one piece box as explained on page 82.

The jug candle stick holder (fig. 96) was made by silver soldering a bowl shaped top section (formed by the beating down method) to a tapered seamed bottom section. The collar, handle, and bottom were soft soldered to the body.

MORE ON SEAMED OBJECTS Seamed cylindrical and tapered objects can have their centers hammered in (concaved) as shown in the object in figure 96A and one or both ends can be flared out as shown in the incompleted object in figure 76.

Fig. 96 Jug Candlestick Holder

figure 98 were made from one piece of metal. The front and back parts were curved, domed out, and then soldered to the other metal to form the body of the pitcher. The spout was made (see fig. 127) and silver soldered to the body. The top and handle were then assembled. The cover was made as shown. The knob and handle were cut from ebony.

The teapot in figure 99 (made from copper) was constructed to explain grooved assembly construction. The body was made as shown in figure 99A. Note that side A is equal to A' and that B equals B'. The metal

Fig. 97 Silver cream pitcher—assembled construction

assembled with soft solder since the pot was constructed from copper. Silver teapots should be assembled with silver solder.

Fig. 96A Silver Coffee Pot by Bernard Bernstein

is first scribed deeply and then grooved with a grooving tool (see fig. 112), bent to a 90° angle and silver soldered. The sides are then curved over a round stake or steel rod. After all sides are grooved, bent, soldered, and the edges are also soldered together, the body is planished. The inside corners of the body can be planished with a hand-made rectangular shaped hammer head:—dimensions of ½″ x ¾″ x 1″. The top of the body was formed by the straight raising process. See figure 127 for the method of forming the spout. The handle was cast in two sections (see casting chapter). The two halves were silver soldered together. All other parts were

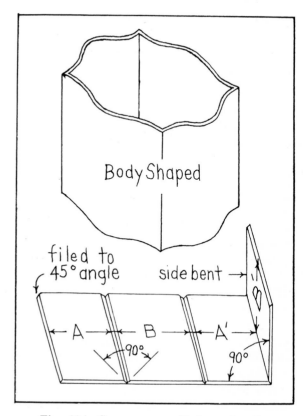

Fig. 99A Groover assembled construction

Fig. 98 Small teapot with ebony handle and knob

Fig. 99 Teapot—assembled construction

PLATE AND TRAY CONSTRUCTION

Plates and trays can be constructed by hand in wood or metal forms or without forms. In schools, camps, and other programs participated in by young craftsmen, the use of a form is advisable. The method that does not require forms is often preferred by creative craftsmen since it doesn't limit the design, shape, and size of the finished plate or tray to the form. Both methods are described below.

1. FORM METHOD

Forms, such as the one shown in figure 100, can be purchased from craft supply houses or, if a lathe is accessible, they can be turned. The preferred wooden forms are made from maple: the metal ones are available in cast aluminum and iron. The commercial forms can be obtained up to a diameter of 10 inches.

REQUIRED METAL The diameter of the required disc should be the same as that of the form. 20 gauge metal can be used for 6″ and smaller plates and trays; 18 gauge is recommended for plates and trays larger than 6″.

Since aluminum is a light metal, thicker gauges can be used.

FORMING PROCEDURE On the metal disc, with a pencil compass, scribe a circle where the metal is to be hammered down to form the plate. Place the disc on the plate form and with a silversmith hammer or mallet shown in figure 100 tap the metal down to form the plate. Hammer the metal just inside the scribed circle. Rotate the metal or move the hammer along after each hammer blow and bring the metal down slowly:— that is, do not attempt to form the plate in one group of blows. When the starting point has been reached after the first circle of blows, continue the process again and hammer the metal down a little more. Repeat the process until the metal is brought down to match the shape of the form. **Note:**—The center of the plate is never hammered down. The required hammering is only done next to the scribed circle.

The entire rim of the plate can be planished or ball peened. This can be done in the form or, better yet, over a flat (bottom) stake or the face of an anvil.

Fig. 100 Hammers, aluminum form, and plates

The center or bottom of the plate also can be planished. Finally, the bottom of the plate must be set so that the plate rests as shown in figure 101-1. In schools or camps, young craftsmen may turn the plate over and hammer the center of the plate up to obtain the required shape so that the plate will not rock. A superior method of setting the bottom of a plate will be explained in the following chapter on plate forming without a form.

2. FREEFORM METHOD

The plate is first designed full-size on paper. The size of the disc of metal to make the plate is the same as the designed plate; however $\frac{1}{8}''$ may be added for trimming purposes. With a divider, scribe a circle where the metal is to be hammered down to form the plate.

FORMING PROCEDURE Place in a vise, with its end grain up, a 2" x 4" or larger piece of wood, preferably maple. The end grain surface of the wood should be flat and

smooth and its edges sharp. Hold the flat disc of metal firmly over the wood block as shown in figure 101-2. Note that the scribed circle where the metal is to drop is directly over the edge of the wood and only the rim of the plate to be formed rests on the wood. Beginners may use two nails to help keep the scribed line directly over the edges of the wood. With a silversmith hammer tap the metal down to start the plate forming operation.

Hammer the metal directly down just inside the scribed circle and after each blow rotate the metal not the hammer. Bring the metal down slowly:—that is, do not attempt to obtain the necessary depth in one group of blows for the metal is apt to crack or stretch unevenly. Continue to hammer the metal down and to rotate the metal until the starting point has been reached.

After the starting point has been reached, hammer the plate down a little further, rotate the metal and continue the process again. Usually a plate can be formed in three or four hammering operations. Anneal and pickle the metal, if necessary, between each hammering.

THE RIM The hammer forming operation, if not done carefully, tends to warp the entire plate, especially the rim. The warping is removed by placing several sheets of newspaper on a smooth surface, preferably a large surface plate, and then placing the plate, rim down, over the paper. A smooth block of wood (2" x 2" x 6" will do) is held, end grain down, as shown in figure 101-4. While an assistant holds the rim of the plate down firmly against the paper, hammer the block around the entire plate until the warp has been eliminated.

SHARPENING THE INNER EDGE OF THE RIM It is important that the plate should drop exactly at the scribed circle in order to get a perfectly round plate. The edge where the rim drops is sharpened by holding the plate over the block of wood and hammering down upon it with a flat faced planishing hammer. Here too, rotate the plate; do not move the hammer.

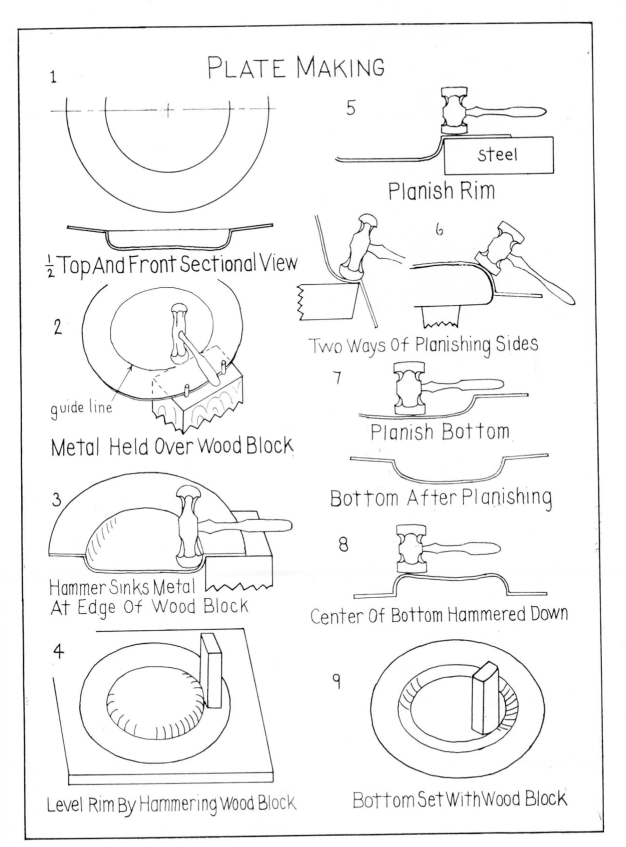

PLATE MAKING

1 ½ Top And Front Sectional View

2 guide line — Metal Held Over Wood Block

3 Hammer Sinks Metal At Edge Of Wood Block

4 Level Rim By Hammering Wood Block

5 steel — Planish Rim

6 Two Ways Of Planishing Sides

7 Planish Bottom — Bottom After Planishing

8 Center Of Bottom Hammered Down

9 Bottom Set With Wood Block

Fig. 101

Fig. 102 A professional silversmith planishing the center of a plate.

If, due to improper hammering, the curved or formed part has been hammered into the rim area it can be corrected by pushing the plate firmly against the wood block and hammering down upon the rim.

If the formed part does not reach the scribed circle, use the silversmith hammer again and hammer the metal down to the scribed line as explained above in the forming procedure.

Now, if the inner edge of the rim is sharp and round and the plate has been formed to the required depth, the plate is annealed, pickled, and finally planished. Before planishing, if necessary, remove any warp from the plate as described above.

PLANISHING THE RIM Remember: The purpose of planishing is to make the metal hard and smooth.

The rim of the plate is planished over a flat steel bottom stake as shown in figure 101-5. Start from the inner edge of the rim and work out to the outer edge. Planish in concentric circle fashion:—that is, hammer around the entire inner edge first, then move the hammer blow out the width of its mark and hammer around again. Repeat by moving the hammer out after each circle is completed until the entire rim is planished.

Note from figure 101-1 that the outer edge of the rim should be slightly higher than the

inner edge. The reason:—if liquid spills on the rim it should flow into the plate and not out. To raise the outer edge of the rim, turn the plate over and with a planishing hammer tap the rim down so that its outer edge is slightly higher.

PLANISHING THE CONCAVED SIDES—

Method A: Hold the plate almost perpendicular to the flat bottom stake as shown in figure 101-6. With a silversmith hammer that matches the inner (concave) shape of the plate, planish the inner top edge. Hammer straight down against the plate and after each blow rotate the plate the width of the hammer mark and continue planishing until the starting point is reached. Then, tilt the plate in slightly (about 5 degrees), move the hammer in the width of the planish mark and continue planishing the metal in a circular fashion again:—and so on until the concave section of the plate is planished.

Method B: The inner top edge is planished as explained above in method A. The rest of the concave section is planished from the outside as shown in figure 101-6. Note that the shape of the stake must match the curvature of the plate as nearly as possible. It is best, when planishing, to start from as near to the rim as possible and to work out

Fig. 103 Pewter Plate—free form method

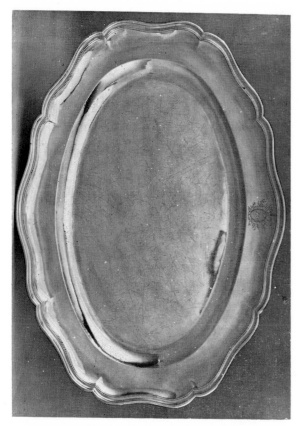

Fig. 104 Platter   Pierre Balzar, French, 1771
Courtesy of The Metropolitan Museum of Art

to the center of the plate, hammering, of course, around in circles.

PLANISHING THE CENTER The center or bottom of the plate is planished over a flat bottom stake as shown in figure 101-7. Start planishing from where the curved sides were planished and gradually, in circular fashion, work in towards the center. Use the widest flat planishing hammer that is available in order to obtain a smooth and hard surface. When planished, the bottom of the plate will appear as shown in figure 101-7. The center of the tray can also be planished from the outside as shown in figure 102. Note the width of the planishing hammer.

SETTING THE BOTTOM Place the plate, face down, upon a surface plate or bench and with a planishing hammer tap the center metal down to the shape shown in figure 101-8. When tapping, start from the center of the plate and, hammering in circles,

work out to the position shown in figure 101-8. Turn the plate face up and have a helper hold the plate, by pressing down on its rim, firmly against the surface plate. It is best first to place several sheets of paper or a piece of leather between the plate and the surface plate.

Shape a piece of wood (2" x 2" x 8") so that its bottom (end grain) is smooth and one edge is curved to the required diameter of the setting position (fig. 101-9). Now hold the wooden setting tool in the position shown in figure 101-9 and hammer it firmly and while hammering move the piece of wood completely around the plate. It is best, with a pencil compass, to scribe a circle on the plate as a guide line for the setting tool.

Check the plate on the surface plate to see if it rests properly. If necessary, repeat the process. A steel setting tool (fig. 75) can be used instead of the wood tool.

OVAL PLATES Oval plates and trays can be made by means of the freeform plate method described above.

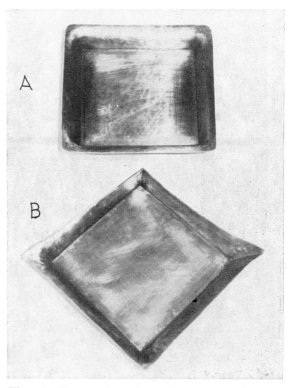

Fig. 106 Tray with convex sides and rounded corners. B: Sample tray showing square corner construction procedure.

3. RECTANGULAR TRAYS

EXAMPLE A: Tray with convex sides and rounded corners (fig. 106—page 77).

REQUIRED METAL The size of the metal required to make the tray is determined from the diagram (fig. 105-1). The length of the metal is equal to the base "A" plus the sides "B" and "C". Since B and C are curved, their true lengths can be found by shaping a piece of wire to the shape of the curve and then by straightening the wire and measuring it. The width of the metal (the same as the length in this case) is found in a similar manner. After the metal has been cut to shape, the base lines, where the sides are to be formed, are scribed into the metal by means of a divider or scriber.

FORMING PROCEDURE The tray is formed over a piece of wood, preferably maple, approximately 2″ x 3″ x any length over 4″. Clamp the wood in a vise, end grain up, and then round the corners of the wood slightly with a file. Hold the metal firmly over the wood block with the scribed line, where the metal is to be bent, directly over the edge of the wood. With a planishing hammer, hammer the sides of the tray down to the shape shown in figure 105-2. Repeat the above on all four sides. The sides are hammered down as close as possible to the corners so that a sharp corner, as shown in figure 106-B, is formed.

Each rounded corner is made by holding the metal firmly down and against a corner of the wood block. With a raising hammer (fig. 105-3) drive the corner metal down. Hammer directly over the corner metal first and then move the hammer blows to the sides to even the metal. It will be necessary to anneal the metal and repeat the process once or twice to obtain the required depth and shape in the corners. Finally, with a planishing hammer, hammer the sides and the top of the corners of the tray to the desired shape. This is done by holding the tray

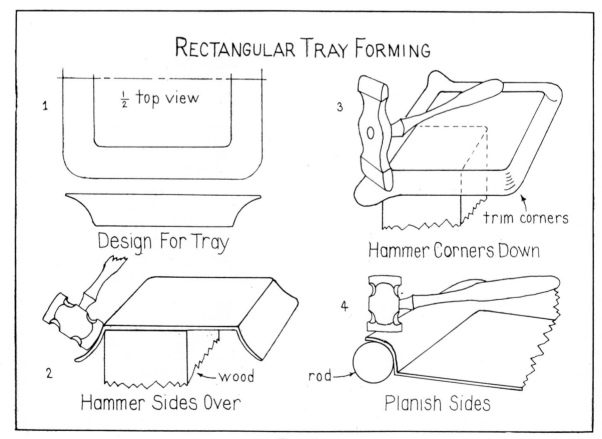

RECTANGULAR TRAY FORMING

1. ½ top view — Design For Tray

2. Hammer Sides Over — wood

3. trim corners — Hammer Corners Down

4. rod — Planish Sides

Fig. 105

Fig. 107 Aluminum ash tray with straight sides and sharp corners

against a round steel rod (fig. 105-4) or a narrow "T" stake.

Note: The metal in the corners becomes longer as the corners are formed. It is best to trim off surplus metal during the forming process.

PLANISHING THE TRAY The bottom of the tray can be planished from the inside and outside over a flat bottom stake. Reread the section on straight raising which describes the technique for forming a sharp edge where the sides of the tray meets the bottom. In a similar manner, the bottom edge of this tray can be planished. The sides of the tray are planished over the stake shown in figure 105-4.

SETTING THE BOTTOM The bottom is set by the same method used for setting the bottom of a plate. In that method the bottom is hammered back slightly from the back, then a block of wood is hammered all around the edge of the bottom next to the sides so that the tray will rest on a table without rocking. Slight corrections also can be made in the bottom edge next to the sides by means of a large line-chasing tool or a small chisel made from brass. **Caution:** Tap the tool lightly and move it along after each blow so as not to hammer a groove into the metal.

After the tray has been planished and the bottom set, the edge of the tray is filed; it is then finished as desired.

EXAMPLE B: Tray with straight sides and sharp corners (fig. 107).

FORMING PROCEDURE By using the method described in example A, a tray can be formed with straight sides and sharp

corners as shown in figure 107 and 106-B. It is easy to obtain the straight sides; just hammer the side metal straight down on the wood forming block (fig. 105-2). The sharp corners can be obtained by using the technique explained in example "A" for forming the corners. With a raising hammer, hammer each corner down and against the wood block. By annealing and repeating the process several times, the sharp corner can be obtained.

Note: The metal in the corners becomes longer as the corners are formed. It is best to trim off surplus metal during the forming process.

PLANISHING THE TRAY The entire tray can be planished over a flat bottom stake by using the technique described in method "A". The corners of the sides are planished and sharpened individually by holding each corner over a corner of the flat bottom stake and then by tapping the corner with a planishing hammer on one side and then the other.

After the tray has been planished, the top edge is filed and then the tray can be finished as desired.

IRREGULAR SHAPES Irregular shaped trays can be formed by means of the techniques already described. The tray shown in figure 107A with convex sides can be formed by hammering the sides down as explained in rectangular trays or the sides can be formed by the straight raising technique (page 55). The corners of the tray were sharpened with a line chasing tool. A border was soldered to the top edge of the tray.

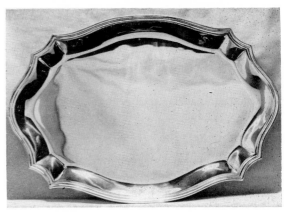

Fig. 107A Silver Tray   **Peruzzi, Florence, Italy**

79

BOX CONSTRUCTION

Box construction in this book is divided into the following construction methods:— elementary, one piece, and assembled. In each case the thickness of the required metal must be determined by the size and use of the box and by the kind of metal (brass, copper, sterling, etc.) that is to be used. It is essential that the box be planned or designed carefully on paper and that the measurements be transferred onto the metal accurately.

Tubing (chenier) for hinged covered boxes can be made as explained in figure 53. The tubing is cut to the required knuckle length with a jeweler's saw. The ends of the knuckles or tubes can be filed perfectly, so that they fit together exactly, as follows: Drill a hole, the exact diameter of the tubing,

through a piece of steel (fig. 108). The tubing is then placed through the hole so that it projects slightly; thus the tubing can be filed perfectly by holding it steady and by filing until the file touches the steel. If tool steel is used, it may be hardened and tempered. It is advisable to make a steel plate with different sized holes for a permanent file plate.

The size of the box depends upon its use. The construction procedure explained below is practically the same for small and large boxes. All parts of sterling silver boxes should be hard soldered together; soft solder can be used on some brass and copper boxes.

ELEMENTARY BOX CONSTRUCTION The elementary box (fig. 108) is made as follows:

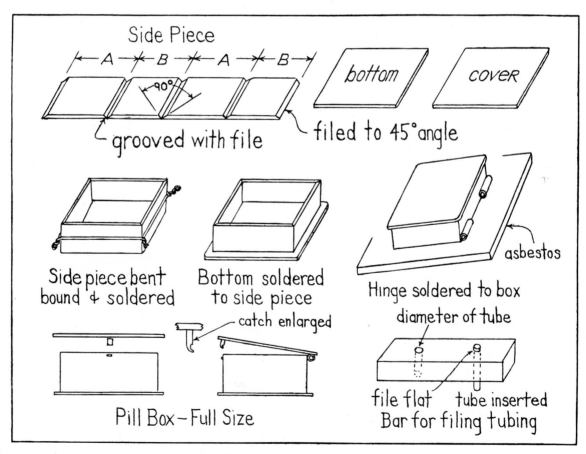

Fig. 108 Elementary Box Construction

The strip for the side piece must be divided into its proper sections carefully. Distance A must equal A and B equal B exactly. The bending positions are first deeply scribed into the metal and then the metal is grooved with a file. The grooving may be started with a three square file and finished with a hand file in order to get the required 90 degree angle. The depth of the groove should almost be the metal's thickness. The ends of the strip are filed to a 45 degree angle. The metal strip is bent by hand to form the sides, bound with binding wire, and then hard soldered together. Note that the binding wire is bent so that each corner gets a twist; thus the strip may be held firmly together. Solder each corner separately.

The soldering can be done by the cut solder method (see soldering) or quickly by the strip method. If the strip solder method is used, the metal is heated to light red, then the solder is touched to the edge of the seam. Remove the torch as the solder flows to avoid overheating and melting the metal.

After soldering and pickling, the sides are evened by hammering lightly with a planishing hammer over a flat stake. The bent strip should now form a perfect rectangle; if not, the smaller side or sides can be stretched slightly by hammering over a flat bottom stake. Sometimes it is advisable to cut the metal straight down one of the corners to shorten one or two sides, and then to re-solder the corner.

The bottom is soldered to the side strip and then the tubing for the hinge is soldered to the box as shown in figure 108. Note that the asbestos board is placed at an angle so that the tubing will roll against the box. The seam of the tubing should touch the box. Use small pieces of solder to avoid filling the hole in the tubing.

A piece of tubing is now cut and filed so that it fits between the box tubing. It is then soldered to the cover to complete the hinge. Three section hinges are satisfactory for small boxes; five and more sections should be used for larger boxes. Note: in order that the joint strength of the cover and the box should be approximately the same, the combined length of the even number of tubes on

Fig. 109 Copper Cigarette Box

Fig. 110 Brass Cigarette Box—cover engraved

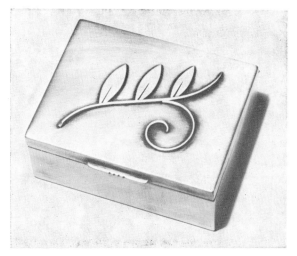

Fig. 111 Silver Cigarette Box

the cover should equal that of the odd number of tubes on the box. The cover is held to the box by inserting a wire (same diameter as the inside of the tube) through all the tubes. The ends of the wire should be filed even with the ends of the outer tubes.

The type of catch shown in figure 108 may be used for pill boxes. Larger boxes usually do not require catches.

Note: The sides (body of the copper box in figure 109 and the brass box in figure 110) were soft soldered to the bottoms. Both boxes have lift covers. The covers are held in position on the boxes by four small right angle pieces made from a strip of 18 gauge metal, 3/16″ by ¾″. The corner pieces can be bent by grooving or by hammering in a vise. They are soft soldered in position.

The copper box in figure 109 can be an excellent school or camp project. A strip of 18 or 20 gauge copper, 12″ long and 1″ wide,

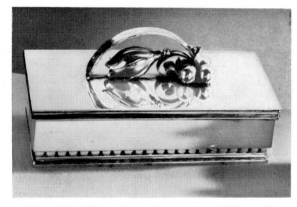

Fig. 111A Silver Box—International Silver Co.

is bent to form a rectangle 2¾″ by 3¼″. The strip can be bent to shape in a brake in a school shop or in pieces of angle iron in a camp or craft shop. The ends of the strip are filed to a 45° angle and then silver soldered. After soldering, the sides are planished, filed, and soft soldered to the bottom —20 gauge metal.

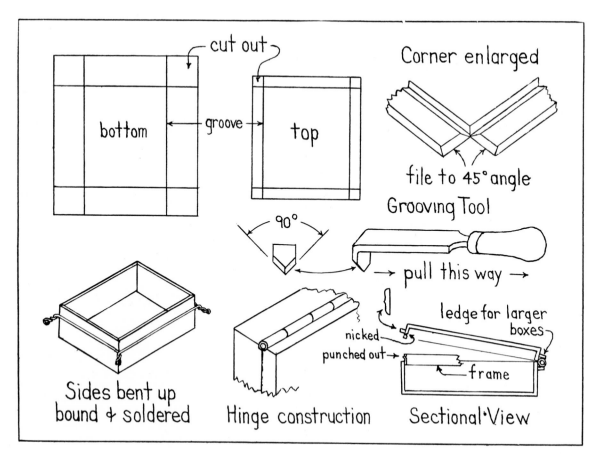

Fig. 112 One piece bottom and top box construction

The cover can be designed as desired. In figure 109, after the cover is planished, the lines are made by rolling the cover through the burring wheels on a sheet metal rotary machine. The leaf is soft soldered to the cover. The cover is crimped by means of a small raising hammer by merely hammering the metal down where desired while the cover is on the box. The bottom is crimped in a similar manner.

The box in figure 110 is made from half-hard brass. The sides are grooved, filed, and bent as explained in figure 108. After bending, all seams and parts are soft soldered together. The design on the cover is formed with engraving tools.

ONE PIECE CONSTRUCTION

A cigarette box (fig. 111) will be used to explain one piece bottom and top box construction. The size and thickness of the required metal depends upon the design and size of the box. It is essential that the inside measurements of the bottom and cover piece (fig. 112) match perfectly. Scribe the lines in deeply and then groove the metal to almost (9/10) its entire thickness.

The grooving tool (fig. 112) can be made from the tang (back) of an old file. Reminder:—after the tang has been bent and ground to shape, it must be hardened and tempered.

After grooving, the corners are cut out with a jeweler's saw and are then filed to a 45° angle. Bend the sides up and together, and then bind with binding wire as shown in the diagram. Solder the corners and permit the solder to flow along the grooved sides so that they too are soldered.

After soldering, a little hammering with a planishing hammer may be required to even the sides and then the top edges are filed. It is best that the top of the cover should be domed up slightly for strength and appearance. This is done by planishing it from the inside over a bench block or flat stake.

The hinge is made as shown in the diagram; the one with the ledge (bearer) is superior for larger boxes. Where a ledge or bearer is not used, it is best to file a groove the width of the tubing into the back of the box so that the tubing has a good contact for soldering and is less obvious.

A three-sided strip of metal will align the

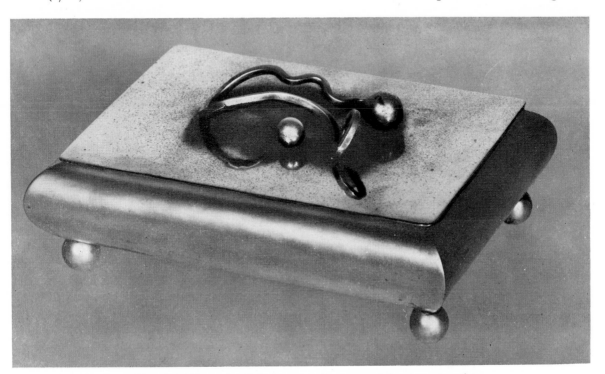

Fig. 113 Silver Jewel Box—one piece curved box construction

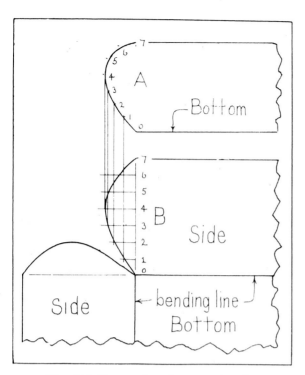

Fig. 114 Corner plan for one piece box

tom box is the box shown in figure 113. The required shape of the flat piece of metal to make the one piece bottom is obtained from the designed curvature of one of the sides (fig. 114). By means of a divider, the side is divided into a number of equal divisions. These divisions are marked off on a line drawn perpendicular to the bottom of the box as shown at B. The correct curvature is obtained by drawing vertical and horizontal lines from the numbers to obtain intersection points. In other words, a vertical line from 1 intersecting a horizontal line from 1' will locate the proper point 1. A vertical line

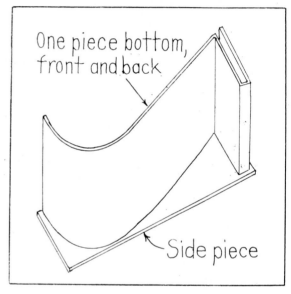

Fig. 115A

top and bottom sections perfectly. The frame is made from one piece of metal, usually 24 gauge. The metal is nicked to form sharp bends and it is placed only along the front and two sides of the box. The snap shown in the sectional view of figure 112 can be used for pill boxes. Larger cigarette boxes do not require snaps.

A different version of the one piece bot-

from 2 intersecting a horizontal line from 2' will locate the proper 2. Do the same for all the numbers. Connect the points to obtain the required curvature. By means of tracing paper and a template, transfer this curvature to all corners of the metal for the box.

Cut the metal to shape with a jeweler's saw and then file the edges of all corners in at a 45° angle. The four sides of the box are bent to shape over a rod and they are then hammered over a bottom stake to form the box. The corners are silver soldered.

Hollow balls are silver soldered to the bottom of the box to form legs. The cover is hinged to the body (11 sections) and is

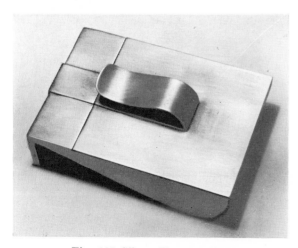

Fig. 115 Silver Cigarette Box

Fig. 116 Silver Cigarette Case

aligned with a frame. The inside edge of the box is also framed.

3. ASSEMBLED CONSTRUCTION

The cigarette box shown in figure 115 will be used to explain the assembled box construction technique.

A rectangular piece of metal is grooved, bent to the shape shown in figure 115A, and then silver soldered where bent to form the one piece back, bottom, and front of the box. To this piece the sides are silver soldered. The sides are cut with a jeweler's saw and then filed to match the shape of the bent piece of metal. The cover and handle are made as shown in the picture.

4. CIGARETTE CASES

The technique of constructing the body of a rectangular cigarette case (fig. 116) is similar to that used to construct the one piece top and bottom cigarette box. Frames, figure 117, are soldered to the top and bottom sections of the case. Note that the bearing for the knuckles of the hinge is formed on the frame. This is best done by grooving the end of the frame metal, bending it down 90°, soldering, and finally tapping the metal over

a thin rod to obtain the required bearing curvature.

The inside of the frame is plotted carefully and cut out with a jeweler's saw. Notches are provided for the catch. The outside of the frame is cut slightly larger than the case; after soldering it is filed flush with the case.

The catch is made as shown in figure 117. If an arm is to be used to hold the cigarettes in place until the case is one half open, metal should be removed from the frame after it has been soldered to the case.

Spring is obtained in the catch by soldering two thin tubes to the case below the frame and then by inserting a piece of a spring into the tubes across the catch as shown in fig. 117.

The case shown in figure 116 has a spring hinge. This is obtained as follows: Use an even number of knuckles (10 in the case shown). Five are soldered to the top of the case, four to the bottom, and one is for the arm. One knuckle must be soldered to the end of the bottom of the case and at the other end the knuckle must be soldered to the top of the case.

A strip of a spring, such as can be obtained from a clock or made from a piece of a thin drill rod, is placed through the hinge to act as a pin. One end of the spring is held with a tapered plug made of silver (fig. 117). With a plier, twist the other end one half turn counter-clockwise and then plug it. Cut the spring and file the ends until flush with the case.

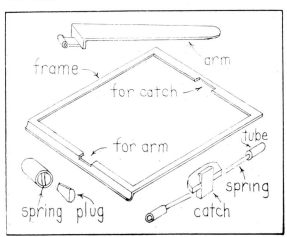

Fig. 117 Parts for cigarette case

SPOONS, PICTURE FRAMES, SPOUTS

1. SPOONS

In Colonial American times, spoons were made by hand in two sections (fig. 119) which were assembled with solder. At present, practically all spoons are forged or rolled and then stamped into shape by means of machines. Several methods of forming spoons by hand are shown in figure 118. Reminder:—design the spoon carefully before starting to make it.

ASSEMBLED CONSTRUCTION In the assembled method, the handle is formed from a rectangular piece of metal. The thickness and width of the metal depends upon the design of the spoon. Often it is best to purchase the metal as thick as the required shank thickness near the bowl and to taper by forging the rest of the shank gradually back to the end of the handle. If the available metal is thinner at the shank than that which is required, the metal can be thickened by carefully hammering its sides together with a planishing hammer. Note that in the assembled construction method the handle is bent to shape over a round bar or stake, notched, and then silver soldered to the formed bowl. The bowl is formed by means of the beating down method over a hollow hammered into a lead block. Use the largest possible forming hammer that matches the required bowl shape in order to avoid nicking the metal. The bowl can be planished over a commercial spoon anvil or, better yet, over one of the forming hammers held in a vise. After the handle has been soldered in position, the bowl and handle are planished lightly to harden the metal; the spoon is then polished.

Figure 118-B illustrates a method of soldering a rectangular wire to a bowl to form a small spoon (fig. 120). Square and other shaped wires can also be used.

ONE PIECE CONSTRUCTION Figure 118-C illustrates the method of constructing a

Fig. 119 Spoons by John Burger about 1790
Courtesy of The Metropolitan Museum of Art

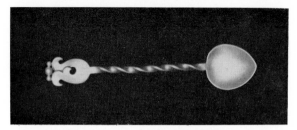

Fig. 120 Small Spoon—assembled construction

Fig. 121 Spoon-Fork—8 to 12 inches long
by Alexandro Solowij Watkins

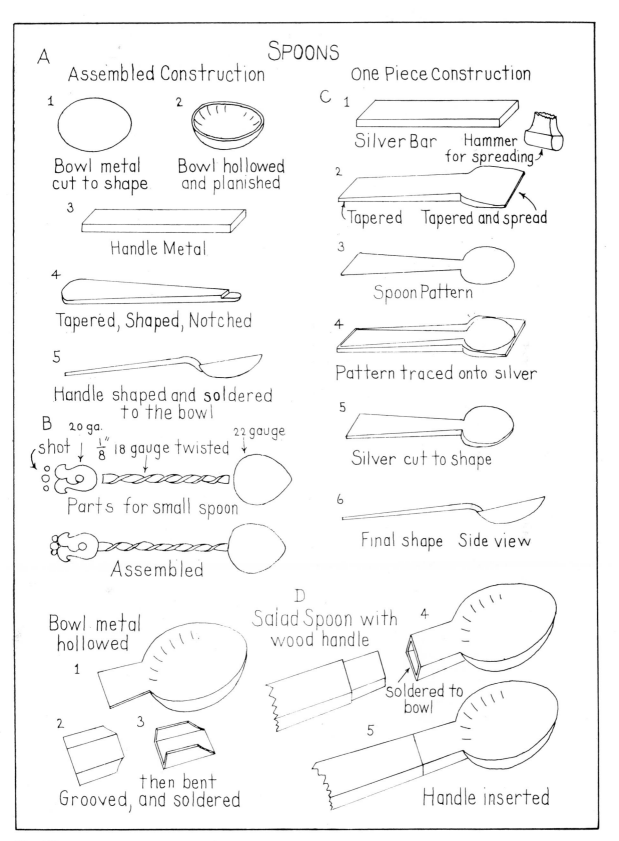

SPOONS

A Assembled Construction

1 Bowl metal cut to shape

2 Bowl hollowed and planished

3 Handle Metal

4 Tapered, Shaped, Notched

5 Handle shaped and soldered to the bowl

B
20 ga. shot | $\frac{1}{8}$" 18 gauge twisted | 22 gauge

Parts for small spoon

Assembled

C One Piece Construction

1 Silver Bar   Hammer for spreading

2 Tapered   Tapered and spread

3 Spoon Pattern

4 Pattern traced onto silver

5 Silver cut to shape

6 Final shape   Side view

D Salad Spoon with wood handle

Bowl metal hollowed

1

2   3 then bent
Grooved, and soldered

4 Soldered to bowl

5 Handle inserted

Fig. 118

spoon (fig. 122) out of one piece of metal. The metal can be purchased as thick as the required shank thickness or slightly thinner. If the metal is purchased thinner, the shank can be thickened by hammering its sides together after the spoon is forged and cut to shape. Remember to allow sufficient metal for thickening purposes.

Note from figure 118-C that the bowl part of the metal can be spread with a raising hammer. The spoon is best forged to shape with a heavy forging hammer on an anvil or a heavy flat stake. Silver can be forged red hot (a light red color is best) much easier than when it is cold. If forged cold, it should be annealed several times to avoid cracking the metal.

The bowl of the one piece spoon is formed similarly to the bowl formed for the assembled spoon:—that is, over a hollow hammered into a lead block. It too is planished over a forming hammer or spoon anvil.

Note the cleverly designed spoon-forks in

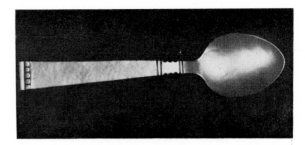

Fig. 122 Spoon—one piece construction

figure 121 which were made without forging from one piece of metal.

Figure 118-D illustrates a method of forming salad servers with wood handles. 18 or 16 gauge metal can be used to form the bowl. Then a piece of metal (18 gauge) is cut, grooved, bent, soldered, and then filed and soldered to the bowl. The handle is filed so that it can be inserted; it can be held in place with a rivet. Ebony was used for the silver salad servers in figure 123. After sand papering, the handles were buffed on a flannel wheel. Wax was applied to the wheel.

Fig. 122A Spoons and fork made by the assembly method—student's work

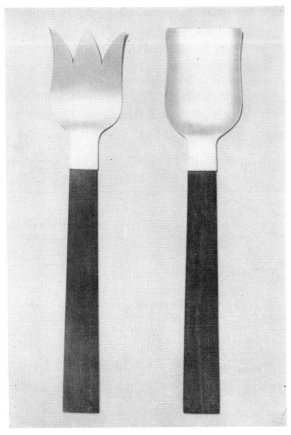

Fig. 123 Silver Salad Servers—ebony handles

Fig. 124 Flatware   Harold A. Milbrath

2. PICTURE FRAMES

Metal picture frames can be formed in several different ways. Frames with flat fronts and sides can be made similarly to the method used for the one piece box construction (see fig. 112). The picture frame shown in figure 125 was made to explain a frame construction technique which is often used for good silver and gold frames.

Note from figure 126 that the frame is formed from one strip of metal. The metal is first bent so that the sides form a 60° angle. The bending can be done in a sheet metal brake or bar folder, in angle iron, or, if a sharp edge is desired, it can be grooved, bent, and silver soldered.

After the metal strip is bent, the part that becomes the front is sectioned and then is notched. Section "A" must equal "A" and "B" must equal "B". Note from figure 126 how the angle for the notch is determined;

Fig. 125 Picture frame—one strip construction

for this frame it is approximately 80 degrees. The notches are cut with a jeweler's saw and the edges are filed straight and in at approximately a 5° angle. The side section then is grooved with a file to about 4/5 of its thickness and its ends are filed at a 45° angle. Then the strip is bent to form a frame, tied with binding wire, and all bends and ends are silver soldered.

The back of the frame is made as shown in figure 126. Note that two small rectangular pieces of metal are soldered to the bottom edge of the frame. The back metal fits into the frame behind these edges and then is held at the top by a pivoting strip of metal.

The glass in the frame will crack if the pressure on it from the back piece is slightly uneven. To equalize the pressure, rubber or cloth strips or tubing are placed around the inside of the frame.

The back support for the picture frame was made from a tapered piece of metal. It was bent to the shape shown and soft soldered to the back piece.

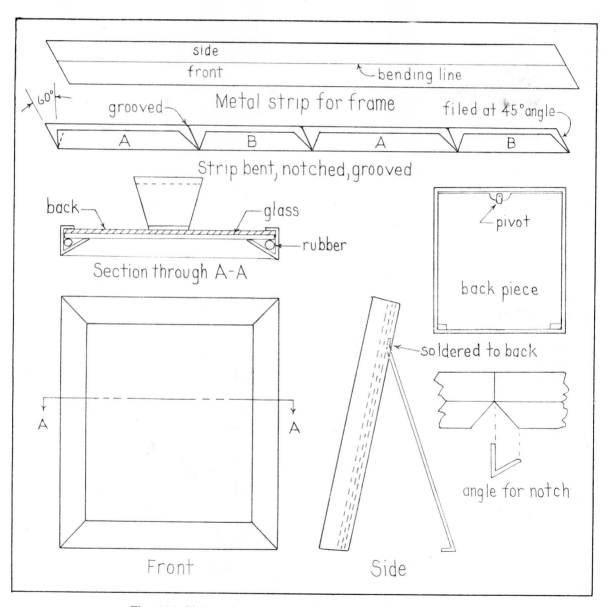

Fig. 126 Picture frame construction—one strip technique

3. SPOUT CONSTRUCTION

Spout construction by hand can be divided into four classifications: namely, straight tapered, tapered and curved, straight fitted, and curved fitted. The four spout types are illustrated in figure 127. Some spouts are cast and this technique is described in the chapter on casting. In all methods of constructing spouts, the design should be drawn carefully on paper and the construction lines must be made directly from the design. The thickness of the required metal depends upon the size and design of the object. 18 and 20 gauge metals often are used.

STRAIGHT TAPERED The straight tapered spout is actually a part of a frustrum of a cone (fig. 56) and can be developed accordingly. One can develop a cone and then can approximate the required contact curvature (0-6X) for the pattern and after the spout has been formed and soldered it can be filed to fit the object.

The actual contact curvature (0-6X) is obtained as follows: First extend the side (A-S) of the spout nearest the object and form a cone. Draw the base circle (the circumference) of the cone (½ required) and divide it into sections 0 to 6 (6 for ½ of the circumference). Distance 0-1 then represents 1/12 of the base circle or the circumference.

Using A-O as a radius, draw line B-B. Mark off distance 0-1 twelve times, 6 on one side of 0 and 6 on the other side. This total distance is the length of the base circle of the cone.

Now from points 1 to 6 draw light lines back to A. Where these line (1″, 2″, 3″, etc.) cross the spout line (0-6″), with a compass and point A as center, draw lines out from them. Finally, from points 1', 2', 3' etc. draw lines back to point A. Where these lines cross the lines from 1″, 2″, 3″ etc. they locate points 2‴, 3‴, etc. Connect these points to form the required actual contact curvature for the spout pattern.

The pattern is traced onto the metal which is then cut to shape. The edges of the metal are filed perfectly straight and in slightly (about 5°) so that when the metal is bent they will meet perfectly. The bending can be done over a narrow round stake by tapping the edges to start the curving process and then by hammering them together,

Fig. 128 Silver Teapot by Paul Revere

The Metropolitan Museum of Art

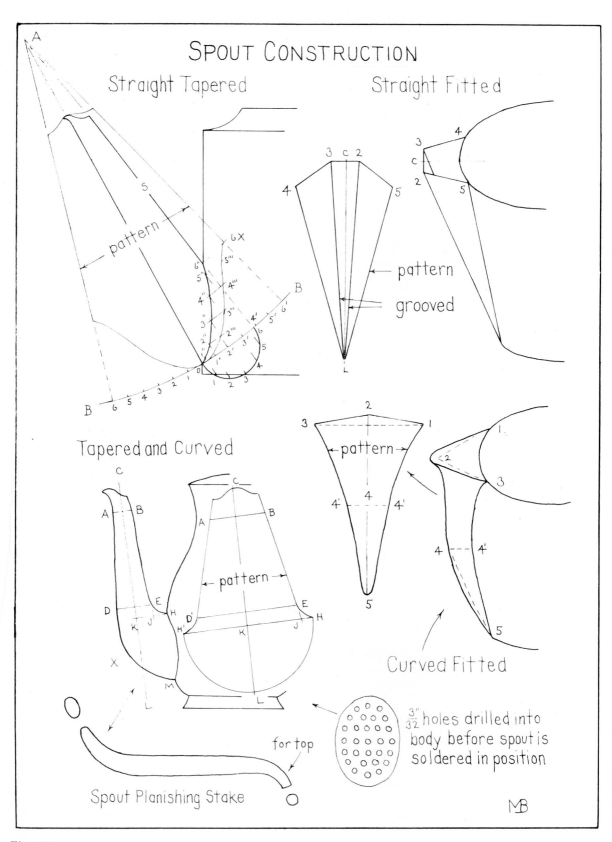

Spout Construction

Straight Tapered

Straight Fitted

pattern

grooved

pattern

Tapered and Curved

pattern

pattern

Curved Fitted

$\frac{3}{32}$" holes drilled into body before spout is soldered in position

for top

Spout Planishing Stake

MB

Fig. 127

92

which can be done on a bench without a stake, to form a perfect joint. After the joint has been silver soldered, the spout is planished. The planishing can be done on a narrow sheet metal or silversmith stake, on a ring mandrel, or by filling the spout with lead or pitch.

TAPERED AND CURVED This spout can be developed and formed from one piece of metal as follows: Draw a center line C-L. Perpendicular to this line, mark the circumference of the spout at A-B and D-E. Since A-B and D-E are diameters, the length of the circumferences will be their distances times 3.14 or 22/7. Connect A to D and B to E. Extend B-E and locate point J. Draw a line perpendicular to the center line through J and locate K and H. With K as center and radius K-H draw a semi-circle, then connect H' to D'. Add the top distances to the spout pattern to complete it.

The metal is cut to the pattern's shape, then its edges are filed and bent similarly to the metal for the straight spout. The edge of the spout from E to H must be hammered together carefully to form a good seam. No attempt at present should be made to shape the metal to the curvature of the spout at D-M.

After the seam has been soldered, the spout at E-H is curved over a narrow raising stake and then the spout is formed to match the shape at D-M. This is done by necking-in (see fig. 87) the metal with a raising hammer over a small domed and also a narrow raising stake. To match the shape at D-M, the metal will have to be annealed several times.

The center of this spout is planished as explained for the straight tapered spout. The top of the spout can be curved and planished on the spout planishing stake. This stake, made from a round or rectangular piece of metal, is forged, filed, and shaped as shown in figure 127. Parts of the bottom of the spout, especially near X, also can be planished on this stake. The rest of the bottom of the spout is planished on a domed and also a raising stake. After planishing, the bottom of the spout is filed with a half round file until it fits the object perfectly.

STRAIGHT FITTED This pattern is developed as follows: Draw a center line C-L and a line perpendicular to it at C. Mark off the distances C-2 and C-3, then connect 2 to L and 3 to L.

Point 5 can be located by tracing on tracing paper the triangle 2-5-L and then by holding the tracing paper on the pattern and marking point 5 onto it. Point 4 is located similarly.

After the metal for the pattern is cut to shape, lines 3-L and 2-L are scribed deeply, grooved (see box construction), bent to shape, and finally silver soldered to complete the spout.

CURVED FITTED The pattern for the curved fitted spout can be determined as follows: Depending upon the size of the spout, draw a line 1/4″ to 3/4″ below 2 perpendicular to the center line. Mark off distances 2-1 and 2-3 on this line. From 2, mark off distances 2-4 and 4-5. At 4, draw a perpendicular line and locate points 4 and 4'. Connect the outer points to complete the pattern.

After the pattern metal is cut, the spout is formed by first bending the metal along the center line; then the metal is curved. The curving can be done from the outside by hammering the metal over a shaped piece of wood or steel or over a curved raising hammer. The metal also can be curved from the inside by hammering from the inside with a curved raising hammer over a grooved piece of wood. After shaping the metal, the metal can be planished over the curved raising hammer or over a shaped piece of steel.

HOLES Before the spouts are soldered into position, a group of holes should be drilled into the object as shown in figure 127. **Note:** —the combined widths of the holes should be greater than the width of the spout at the pouring end to permit an even flow of liquid. Dip a pencil into oil to obtain a dark line, and mark the position of the holes carefully. Mark where the holes are to be drilled with an engraving tool or an awl so that they are drilled exactly where desired.

DECORATIVE PROCESSES

1. CHASING AND REPOUSSÉ

Chasing and repoussé are the terms used to describe the process of applying ornamentation and of modeling sheet metal by means of steel tools. Chasing is that phase of the work that is done from the front or top side of the metal; repoussé is done from the reverse or back surface. The tools used are known as chasing tools and the metal is held in a substance known as pitch or over a lead block or a piece of wood.

CHASING TOOLS Chasing tools can be purchased from many jewelry supply houses. It is suggested, however, that the tools be made. Since 50 or more tools are required for professional work (fig. 130) it is best to make a few of the fundamental shapes first and add other shapes as the need arises.

The tools (fig. 131) may be divided into the following categories:

TRACERS OR LINERS As the name indicates, these tools are used for forming lines, straight or curved, on metals. The tools are filed to the shapes shown in figure 131. Note they do not cut through the metal but merely indent it.

EMBOSSING OR DOMING These tools are used for raising metal, generally from the back or reverse side. Some of the tools are round, others are rectangular, but all have smoothly rounded edges so that they will not cut or nick the surface of the metal.

PLANISHING OR SMOOTHING These tools are used to smooth (planish) the metal from the top surface. The working faces of the tools are perfectly flat with the exception of the square ones, which have slightly rounded edges. These tools when used properly, impart to the metal a pleasing texture that makes good chased work so desirable.

MATTING OR BACKGROUND These tools are used to give fine dotted or cross-lined effects on depressed or lowered surfaces. They are often used on the background metal of small transparent glazed objects and on the depressed surface of etched metal work.

DAPPING AND HOLLOW PUNCHES Dapping punches are round punches used to form spherical shapes on metals. The metal is punched from the reverse side and the hollow punch is then used on the front side to form a perfect spherical shape. Hammer the tool lightly to avoid cutting through the metal. Large dapping punches can be made from wood.

HOW TO MAKE CHASING TOOLS Required: Square tool steel bars, 3/16″ wide for most liners and planishers; 1/4″ square bars for the slightly larger tools; 3/8″ and larger bars and rods for the few required large embossing or doming tools. Use round rods for the round doming tools. Round tool steel

Fig. 130 Professional chaser working on a bowl

94

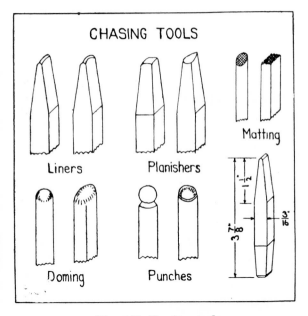

CHASING TOOLS

Liners

Planishers

Matting

Doming

Punches

Fig. 131 Chasing tools

rods may be used for the small liners and planishers; however, they tend to slip and turn, whereas the square tools will not. Cut the steel to 3-⅞″ lengths with the exception of the larger embossing tools which should be cut 4-½″ long.

A straight tracer is made from 3/16″ sq. bar 3-⅞″ long, as follows: Starting 1-½″ from one end, taper the steel as shown in figure 131 to 1/16″; then file to the edge (a blunt cold chisel one) shown in the enlarged view. Note that the tool is rounded very lightly at the ends so that the tool when used will slip along the metal and not cut into it. After filing, polish the tool, especially the edge, with very fine emery paper. Harden the edge (see hardening and tempering) and then temper to a dark straw color to complete the tool. If a better appearing and balanced tool is desired, taper the four top sides as shown in the diagram and then chamfer them slightly. It is best to do the filing in a vise.

The other liners are made in a somewhat similar manner; however, smaller, larger, and even curved edged ones may be required. The planishers, embossing, etc., can be figured out from the diagram.

Occasionally it is necessary to forge some of the tools, especially the embossing ones,

to flatten and widen the steel. This is done by heating the steel to cherry red and hammering it while it is still red on an anvil or heavy piece of steel. After the steel is forged and then cooled slowly, it is filed to shape.

CHASING HAMMERS The hammers (fig. 130) have broad flat faces and long thin-necked handles to give the tool elasticity for rapid hammering. The 1″ face hammer is popular. A ball peen hammer can be used if a chasing hammer is not available.

PITCH Pitch is the ideal compound as a base or support material for chasing and repousseing metal. It is sufficiently hard to retain the general shape of the metal, yet it can quickly be softened in spots for the metal to give only in those spots under the chasing tool. It is adhesive, elastic, and easy to apply and remove.

If quantities up to five pounds are required, it is suggested that the pitch be purchased prepared from a reliable supply house. The actual making of pitch is a messy job; however, it is economical to make large quantities.

Fig. 132 Professional worker chasing a pitcher
Courtesy of Samuel Kirk and Son

95

Fig. 133 Plate being chased in pitch

Pitch is composed of:
    Pitch .... 2 pounds
    Plaster of Paris .... 3 pounds
    Tallow .... 2 ounces

Burgundy pitch is preferred for preparing chaser's pitch. It can be purchased from chemical supply houses. Plaster of Paris hardens the pitch, whereas tallow (common candles will do) tends to soften it. Lard oil may be substituted for the tallow. In the winter, tallow may be added to the pitch to keep it soft; in the summer, more plaster of paris may be added to harden it. The pitch is best

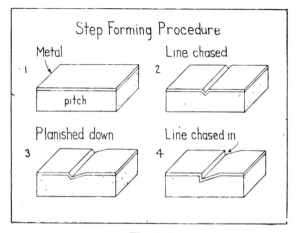

Fig. 134

prepared in an old pail. Warm the green pitch slowly until it melts, and then, while mixing continuously, slowly add the plaster of paris and then the tallow.

HOLDING THE PITCH The ideal form for holding pitch for chasing small metal objects is the chaser's pitch bowl (fig. 132). The bowls are made from cast iron to give them weight, come in 6″ and 8″ diameters, and are set on a cord or leather ring base or a pillow so that they may be placed in any convenient position for good chasing. Avoid the thin metal bowls:—they are too light and vibrate annoyingly when used, and their edges are too sharp.

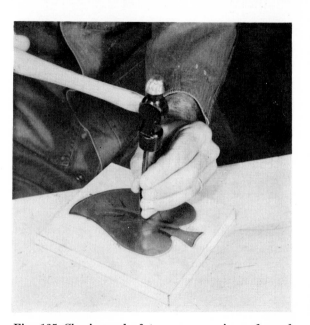

Fig. 135 Chasing a leaf tray over a piece of wood

Metal pie pans, round and rectangular, and other household metal pans (fig. 133) can be used by craftsmen. Framed rectangular blocks of wood with pitch piled on top can be used for large objects. Pitch can also be softened and poured into vases and pitchers. Before pouring the pitch some craftsmen place the largest possible rectangular piece of wood in the vase or pitcher.

PLACING THE METAL IN THE PITCH Oil the back or inside surface of the metal object to be chased in order to prevent the

Fig. 136 Chased Loving Cup   Samuel Kirk and Son

pitch from adhering when it is removed after the chasing operation is completed. Heat the surface of the pitch slowly, moving the torch (use a large flame with little air) continuously to avoid burning the pitch. When the pitch is sufficiently soft, drop the metal on it and then wiggle the metal sidewards to remove air pockets underneath. Raise some of the pitch over the edge of the metal to hold it down firmly while chasing. The pitch now can be cooled quickly by placing the bowl under a running cold water faucet.

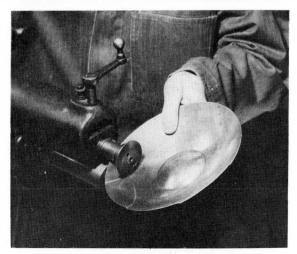

Fig. 137 Burring wheels forming a
rolled "chased" line

CHASING AND REPOUSSÉ PROCEDURE

The actual chasing and repoussé procedure is comparatively easy. Patience, common sense and artistic ability are the important requisites.

STRAIGHT LINES Straight lines are formed by means of a straight liner or tracer. Hold the tool as shown in figures 132 and 133 with the small and fourth finger resting on the metal to keep the tool from slipping. Incline the tool back about five degrees and then strike the tool lightly with a hammer. Repeated hammer blows will move the tool forward to form a sharp straight line. The

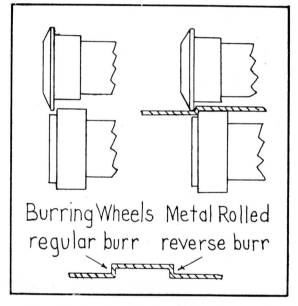

Fig. 138 Burring wheels and how they work

depth of the chased line varies with the force of the hammer blow.

CURVED LINES Most curved lines are also formed with straight liners or tracers. Use a tool with a small and slightly rounded edge. Hold the tool as described above; however, while hammering the tool twist it gradually to form the curved line.

RAISED OR DOMED SURFACES Raised or domed surfaces are formed from the back of the object. First, on the front, line-chase all necessary outlines. Then, remove the object

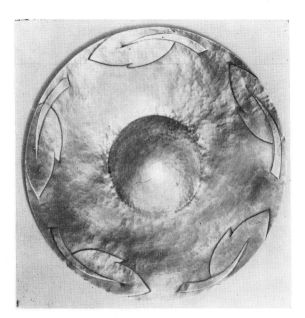

Fig. 139 Bowl—design rolled on

from the pitch, anneal it if necessary, and replace it in the pitch, back side up. Finally, use doming or embossing punches or hammers to raise the metal. The metal may then be reversed again and chased from the front.

TO FORM STEP EFFECTS (fig. 134) Step effects are formed by first line-chasing the object where the step is desired. The metal is lowered on one side of the chased line with a flat planishing tool with slightly rounded edges. Hammer the tool rapidly and move it continuously to avoid nicking the metal.

The line-chasing tool is again employed, this time inwards at an angle at the bottom of the step. Often the metal is reversed on the pitch and shaped from the back.

REMOVING THE METAL FROM THE PITCH The metal is removed from the pitch by warming the pitch slightly with a large soft flame. Pick out small metal objects from pitch with an old tweezer and then the pitch can be wiped off. However, on many small objects, it is easier to remove the pitch by heating the metal to a light red for at that temperature the pitch will burn off the metal and turn into a white ash. The metal is also annealed by the light red heat and after cooling, the original color of the metal can be restored by pickling.

Pitch can be removed from large metal objects by warming the object so that the pitch can be wiped off. Gasoline, turpentine, and benzine will dissolve pitch.

LEAD AND WOOD BLOCKS Small metal objects, such as leaves and flat objects that are to be line-chased (fig. 135), can be chased over lead and wood blocks. The lead and wood will give slightly under the chasing tool; however they are sufficiently hard to maintain the shape of the object.

BURRING MACHINE In schools and other shops where a rotary burring machine is available, a design with a step-chased line effect can be rolled onto a metal object (fig. 137).

The burring wheels are set so that the top wheel just overlaps and is lower than the top edge of the bottom wheel (fig. 138). Note from figure 138 that the step effect is obtained and that the metal is lowered towards the bottom wheel. By putting the wheels on the machine the reverse way, the metal can be lowered on the opposite side as shown in figure 138. When reversing the burring wheels, it is necessary to use a split wire ring or washer to compensate for the keyway on the shaft.

Fig. 139A Tray by Rabajes

Fig. 140 Etched Copper Plate

2. ETCHING

Etching is a method of applying ornamentation or a monogram to a metal by means of an acid and an acid resisting varnish. Etching is used primarily by metal craftsmen as a simple, inexpensive means of decorating a metal, and when done properly, etched objects such as trays, plaques, and book ends, can be very attractive.

Black asphaltum varnish is the substance (resist) usually applied to the metal. All parts of the metal not covered by the varnish will be "attacked" and removed by the acid and for that reason the edge and back of a flat object must be covered too. The design may be eaten into the metal by applying the varnish to the surface around it, or the design may be left raised (in relief) by varnishing it only and removing (etching) the metal around it. For copper and brass, nitric acid is used in the proportion of:

1 part acid to 2 parts water, by volume

For aluminum, hydrochloric acid is used in the proportion of:

1 part acid to 2 parts water, by volume

Caution: When preparing the solution, pour the water into the mixing container first and then the acid into the water, for if the acid is poured first it is apt to spatter when water is added. The acid solution may be stored in a glass container or crock.

Etching Procedure

1. Clean the metal to be etched thoroughly. Steel wool can be used.
2. Transfer the design to the metal.
3. With a small brush, paint parts that are to be raised with the black asphaltum-varnish. If the varnish is too thick, thin with turpentine. Keep the brush soft by dipping it occasionally into turpentine.
4. Paint the edge and back surface of a flat object. It may be necessary to permit the top surface to dry before painting the back. The back may be covered with bee's wax by warming the metal slightly and then rubbing the wax over it.
5. Allow the varnish to dry thoroughly before placing into acid. At least four hours are required.
6. Examine the object for exposed metal surfaces. They may be touched up quickly by applying melted bee's wax with a fine brush.
7. Undesirable paint spots may be removed from parts to be etched by scratching with a knife or scratch awl. Edges may be straightened in a similar manner.

Fig. 141 Coaster painted with asphaltum

Fig. 142 A small fluted bowl

strength of the acid and the required etched depth.

10. Remove the object from acid with copper or brass tweezers and then wash in water. If etch is not deep enough, return object to acid. **Note:** When the desired etched depth has been reached, interesting matted effects can be procured by dropping the object into a more concentrated acid solution for a few minutes.

11. To remove asphaltum, place object on newspaper, pour a small amount of turpentine over, rub with steel wool, and then wipe dry with a cloth or newspaper.

8. Slide object into the acid carefully and observe small bubbles which appear. If acid solution is too weak, none or very few bubbles will appear and more acid should be added. If the acid solution is too strong, a brown gas (nitrogen tetroxide) will appear; the reaction will be too violent and will tend to peel the varnish, and more water should be added to weaken the solution.

9. Approximately one to three hours are required for a satisfactory etched depth. The difference in time will be due to the

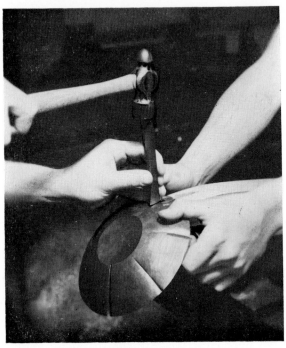

Fig. 144 Fluting a copper bowl

Slight imperfections may be touched up by means of engraving tools. The background may be given a matted effect with standard matting tools. The object can be completed with a high polish or antique finish.

CAUTIONS

Treat acid burns immediately with cold water and soap or bicarbonate of soda.

Keep turpentine away from a flame.

Do not inhale gas fumes (nitrogen tetroxide). Do the etching in a well-ventilated room.

Fig. 143 Line chaser, fluting stake, and a method of marking flutes

Fig. 144A Cream Pitcher—blocked in corners

3. FLUTING

Most fluting of bowls, plates, etc., can be done with a large line-chasing tool, the tip of which is rounded slightly so that it will not cut through the metal. Occasionally, a light raising hammer can be used advantageously.

FLUTING BOWLS A fluting stake is made from a piece of hard wood (maple) which is cut and filed to match the inner curvature

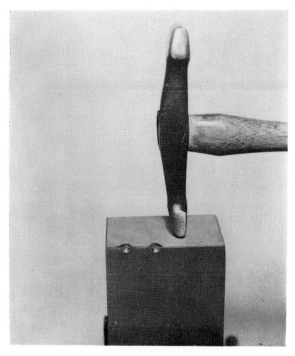

Fig. 145 Wood block notched for crimped edges

of the bowl. A groove is then filed or carved into the wood as shown in figure 143. Note that the groove is deeper and wider in the center of the wood than it is at the end.

The bowl is best marked for fluting by means of a thin strip of metal as shown in figure 143. When fluting, a helper holds the bowl over the fluting stake as shown in figure 144. Start from the edge of the bowl and work in towards the center. The tool is not lifted from the metal; it is pushed towards the center by means of the hammer blows.

Fig. 146 Bowl being crimped with raising hammer

The flute is usually deeper at the edge and gradually lighter at the center.

PLATES Rims of plates (fig. 140) can be fluted over a flat piece of wood with a groove filed into the wood. Plates may be fluted from the top or bottom of the rim.

PITCH To flute vases, pitchers, and other deep objects where wood fluting stakes can not be used, it is best to fill the object with pitch.

OTHER EFFECTS Many other fluted or blocked in effects (fig. 144A) can be given

101

to metal objects after they have been formed by using shaped wood or cast iron or steel forms.

CRIMPED EDGE A crimped edge can be formed quickly on the edge of a bowl or plate with a raising hammer. A piece of wood, end grain up, is notched with a half round file (fig. 145) and the crimping is done over the notch as shown in figure 146.

Note from figure 146 that the metal is held at an angle of approximately 45 degrees to the wood block and that the face of the hammer strikes the metal in a horizontal position.

4. CASTING

Several parts of silver and art metal objects such as heavy irregularly shaped spouts and hollow handles, heavy borders for trays, and handles for cream pitchers and sugar bowls are often made by casting. The metal parts are cast in a very fine sand known as "French" sand or Albany No. 00 sand.*

NOTES ON CASTING In all casting methods, reproductions are made from a model. The model must be made accurately and slightly larger than the desired casting, for allowances must be made for metal shrinkage and for filing and polishing.

The models can be made from wood, plaster of paris, modeling wax, and from metal.

Silver and brass for castings can be melted in graphite crucibles (fig. 147) in furnaces available in many school shops. If a furnace is not available, the metal can be melted with a large torch in the Burno type of hand crucible (fig. 147) obtainable from dealers.

Keep water away from molten (melted) metals. Water hitting the hot metal will form steam and the metal will spatter. It is advisable to wear safety goggles when melting metals.

* The centrifugal or lost wax method of casting is also used for casting silver and art metal objects, especially for intricate small castings. This method is described in the author's book "Jewelry Making for Schools, Tradesmen, and Craftsmen".

Fig. 147 Hand crucible, small furnace, and graphite crucible.

After casting, pickle all objects to remove oxides and foreign matter.

PREPARING THE SAND The dry sand is mixed (tempered) with a light automobile oil or water to hold it together. Properly tempered sand when squeezed in one's hand

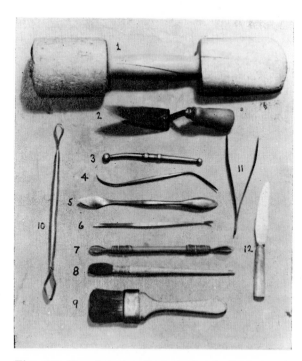

Fig. 148 Foundry (casting) tools: 1. Rammer, 2. Trowel, 3. Beading tool, 4. Slick, 5. Spoon slick 6. Fine swab brush, 9. Dusting brush, 10. Gate cutter, 11. Tweezer, 12. Knife

Fig. 149 Cope around two piece model

Fig. 150 Sand packed around model

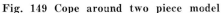

should not ooze water or oil and then when broken in half by hand should part sharply. The sand can be kept in a wooden box or bin or it can be stored in a metal container. A cover will keep the sand from drying.

Water must be added constantly and mixed thoroughly with the sand to keep it properly tempered; oil will not evaporate from the sand and therefore should be added only occasionally. Water tempered sands are superior; oil sands are good for schools—more on this later.

The sand is packed into a flask. The flask has two parts: one with pins, the drag; one with holes to receive the pins, the cope. Packing is best done on a flat piece of steel or marble—called the mold surface.

The method of casting a two piece hollow handle will be explained. It should be comparatively easy with the following information to cast practically all other items required for silver and art metal objects.

Place the cope section of the flask, hole side down, on the mold surface, and then place the two piece model handle in position as shown in figure 149. Now pack the sand into the flask.

The sand is sifted through a sieve or riddle, when packing, in order to remove all foreign matter and to get a fine layer of sand around the model. Ordinary screening can be used to make a riddle. Sift a sufficient amount of sand to completely cover the model and then add unsifted sand until it is several inches above the height of the cope. Now pack the sand firmly into the cope, first with your fingers, especially in the corners, and then with the wedge part of a rammer (fig. 148) and finally with the flat (called butt) end of the rammer. If a rammer is not available a mallet can be used. Smooth the sand by running a flat piece of steel over the top of the cope.

Note: The sand must be packed or rammed properly. If rammed too loosely, the sand is weak and is washed into the casting when

Fig. 151 Drag section being packed with sand

the metal is poured; if rammed too hard, the porosity of the sand is lost so that the air left in the impression made by the model in the sand will not escape quickly enough when the metal is poured:—thus causing defects in the casting. The knack of ramming is easily developed with practice.

To proceed with the casting:—turn the cope over after it has been packed and with a slick (a small spoon can be used) remove the sand between the two halves of the hollow handle model as shown in figure 150. Dust a light layer of prating powder (obtainable from supply houses, though talc powder can be used) over the sand and the model. It is best to keep the powder in a small, semi-porous cloth bag. By tapping the bag lightly it is easy to spread a thin, even layer of powder. The powder acts as a separator:—that is, it prevents the sand in the cope from sticking to the sand in the drag.

Now place the drag part of the flask on the cope, sieve some sand into it (fig. 151), and finally pack it entirely with sand and

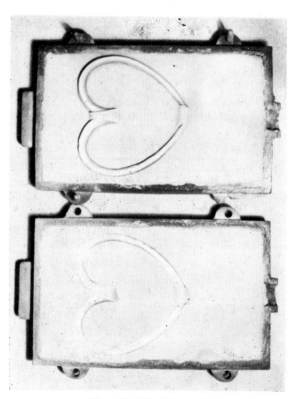

Fig. 152 Flask Parted

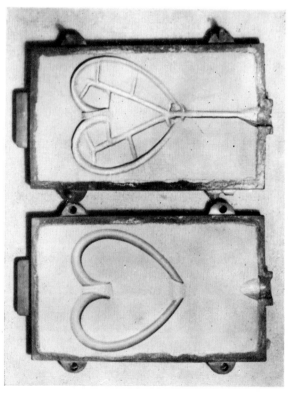

Fig. 153 Model removed, gates cut into sand

Fig. 154 Flask assembled and clamped

The actual casting process is simple. The metal may be melted in a hand or furnace crucible. The hand crucible shown in figure 147 can be used for small castings. The graphite crucible shown in figure 147 is the type used in schools and industrial plants for melting large amounts of silver and brass. When melting silver, some casters add a little poured borax to the crucible to prevent excessive oxidation of the silver. Pour the molten metal as quickly as possible into the gate in the sand. The flask can be opened almost immediately to remove the casting. The gates are nipped or cut off with a jeweler's saw. A little filing is all that should be required to complete most sand cast objects.

To keep molten silver from cooling and thus solidifying too quickly in the crucible after the crucible has been removed from the furnace and before it is poured, the following professional technique may be used: —on top of the silver, before it is melted, place a heavy piece of flat steel. 2 or 3 pieces of 1″ square stock may be used. The steel

after it has been rammed, smooth the top with the aid of a flat piece of steel.

The flask must now be separated and the two piece hollow handle model removed. To separate, tap the sides of the flask lightly with a hammer to vibrate the model and thus remove adhering sand from it. Then slowly remove the drag from the cope. The two halves of the flask will appear as shown in figure 152. The model is removed by turning the cope over so that it can fall out. A sharp impression of the two halves of the model should remain in the sand as shown in figure 153. Finally, gates (sometimes called runners) are cut into the sand with a gate cutter as shown in the upper part of figure 153. A gate cutter is a thin piece of metal bent to form a "U" shaped trough (see fig. 148).

Note that the gates are cut into the drag or back part of the model's impression only. Note too that the gate or runner should be slightly narrower where it touches the model's impression in the sand. The reason:— narrower gate metal can easily be cut from the casting.

The flask is now assembled by first blowing out any loose sand and then clamping it together between two pieces of flat metal or wood as shown in figure 154.

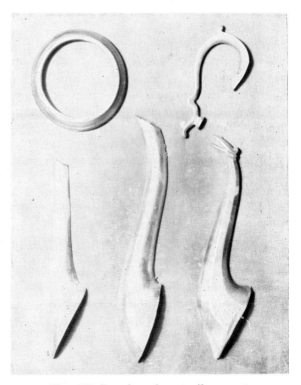

Fig. 155 Samples of cast silver parts

can cover up to ¾ of the opening (top) of the crucible. On top of the steel, place a batch of damp sand to completely cover the opening of the crucible.

Now melt the silver in the furnace. The steel and the sand (the sand hardens into a mass) will float on top of the silver, thus insulating it. To pour the silver into the flask, first push the sand and steel mass a little away from the pouring edge.

The finest castings are procured from dried, water tempered sands. After the flask has been assembled it is baked in a gas oven or over a gas stove until all the moisture in the sand evaporates. Whereas a wet sand will form steam when the molten metal enters and the steam will interfere with the castings, a dry sand will not and therefore a better casting can be had. If time is a factor, good castings can be obtained by merely heating the sand for a moment or two before the flask is assembled.

SILVERSMITHING AND ART METAL PROJECTS AND THEIR CONSTRUCTION

The designing of usable and salable metal objects is a highly specialized branch of the silversmithing and art metal industry. Large manufacturing concerns employ their own designers. Smaller concerns may use the services of independent designers or they may interpret existing designs and vary them slightly to create "original" pieces.

Silversmithing and art metal designs, just as clothing and furniture, are subject to style trends and do change periodically. Contemporary art and fashion often influence the vogue in silversmithing and art metal objects.

New techniques and materials, such as centrifugal casting and modern plastics also can influence commercial designs.

It is essential that all silversmithing and art metal workers—commercial, hand craftsmen, and at schools — give considerable thought to the design of the silversmithing and art metal objects which they make, for an object is only as good as its design. Good design is not restricted to machine or handcraft. A silversmithing or art metal object made by hand or machine may be well or poorly designed. If an object is made by hand and is designed poorly it can be a piece of junk; if an object is made by machine and is designed well it can be a work of art, and vice versa. In other words, the design of the object, not necessarily the method of making it, is the important esthetic consideration.

The Sterling Silversmiths Guild of America is to be praised for stimulating interest in sterling silver design by offering monetary awards and recognition to students of

Fig. 156 Teapot   John Coney, 1700
Courtesy of The Metropolitan Museum of Art

106

Fif. 157 Teapot designed by Richard R. Bruning
Courtesy Sterling Silversmiths Guild of America

design at schools and colleges.

The silversmithing and art metal objects described on the following pages have been selected to help beginning craftsmen at schools, colleges, camps, and home craft shops. Most—not all—are original projects. All, however, have been made and tested with students. To beginners they can offer opportunities for developing useful techniques so that eventually they can design their own objects. Advanced craftsmen and tradesmen, it is hoped, can acquire useful information by observing the design trends of contemporary silver objects submitted by recognized silversmiths.

The cost of materials was considered in designing the objects on the following pages. Wherever possible, the dimensions of projects suitable for school and camp purposes were altered so that standard sizes could be used. For instance, copper is purchased in 8 and 12 inch widths. Therefore, in order to eliminate expensive waste metal, a piece of metal 4 by 8 inches would be used, not a piece 4¼ by 8¼ inches.

FOUR TRAYS

All four trays were made by the beating down method described in figure 66. From the pictures, individual craftsmen can develop their own patterns. The metal may be copper, brass, or silver.

FREE FORM TRAY (fig. 159)

Many contemporary free form shaped trays can be made by means of the "beating down" technique. Figure 158 shows several suggested shapes. The tray in figure 159 was made from number 1. A ¼″ x 1″ diameter ring was soldered to the base of the tray.

The notches in the tray for holding cigarettes were cut to shape with a jeweler's saw.

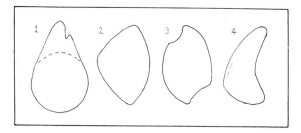

Fig. 158 Suggested free form shapes for trays

Fig. 159 Free Form Tray

ROUND CIGARETTE TRAY (fig. 160)

Tray: 4″ diameter circle, 20 gauge
Handle: ¼″ x 4″, 18 gauge
Holders: ½″ x ¾″, 20 gauge

The tray is hammered to a depth of 1″, planished, and then a base (1¼″ dia.) is formed as described in figure 68.

The handle is planished, shaped with pliers, then soft soldered to the tray.

Grooves are filed into the tray with a half-round file for the cigarette holders. The holders are bent as shown in figure 161; then they are soft soldered in place.

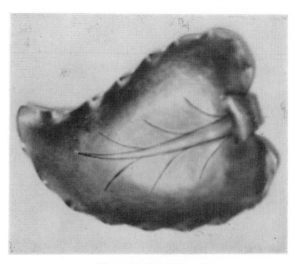

Fig. 162 Leaf Tray

Fig. 160 Round Cigarette Tray

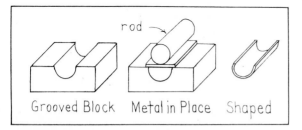

Fig. 161 Method of bending cigarette holder

LEAF TRAY (fig. 162)

The tray was made from sheet metal 4″ x 6″. The metal was cut to shape with shears and the jeweler's saw. The lines are chased in as explained in figure 135.

After the tray has been formed, the edge is crimped as explained in figure 145. The handle is bent over a ¾″ rod.

SILVER TRAY (fig. 163)

Good craftsmenship is warranted when working with silver. All parts of the tray are silver soldered together.

A 4″ diameter, 20 gauge circle was formed into a tray 1¼″ deep. Base:—a 3″ ring was made from 10 gauge square wire 9½″ long. To the top of the base ring, a slightly domed 2⅞″ diameter, 20 gauge circle was soldered. An 8 sided center support was made by grooving, bending, and soldering a 3/16″ x 2½″ strip of 20 gauge silver. Cigarette holders: ½″ x ⅝″, 18 gauge. Holder supports:— 5/16″ x 2¼″, 20 gauge.

Fig. 163 Silver Ash Tray

COAL BUCKET

Many diversified elementary techniques are required to make the coal bucket; this makes it an ideal project for beginners especially in school shops.

MATERIAL   **copper or brass**

1 piece	24 gauge	5" x 8"
1 wire	18 gauge	14" long

PROCEDURE

1. Transfer pattern to metal.
2. Cut metal to shape with straight and curved shers.
3. Bend for grooved seam, shape over stake, and groove (fig. 59).
4. Top of bucket is shaped over stake.
5. Bottom is domed and planished. It is held to bucket with binding wire when soldered.
6. All parts are soft soldered together.
7. Handle is made by twisting 18 gauge wire by means of a hand drill.

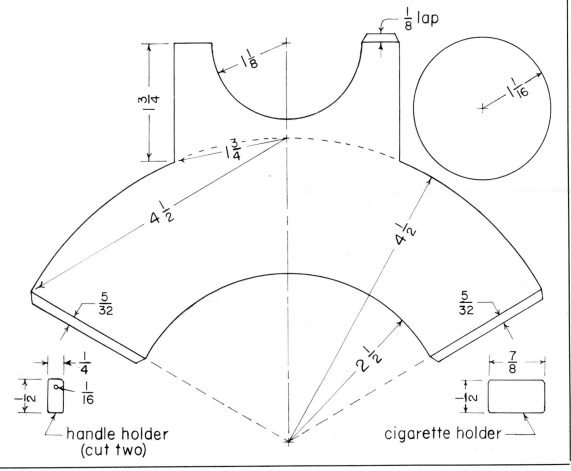

handle holder
(cut two)

cigarette holder

Fig. 164

CIGARETTE HOLDER
and ASH TRAY

This is an excellent project for beginning students in elementary art metal classes. The project contains simple forming and bending operations. The tray can be enameled.

MATERIAL   **copper**

     1 piece   18 gauge $2\frac{1}{4}$″ x $8\frac{1}{2}$″
     1 piece   20 gauge $3\frac{1}{4}$″ x $3\frac{1}{4}$″

Note: 20 gauge brass may be used if the tray is not to be enameled.

PROCEDURE

1. The metal for the holder is planished where indicated. After planishing, tap the metal on the side opposite where planished over a slightly hollowed piece of wood so that the planished surface is domed up slightly (1/16″).

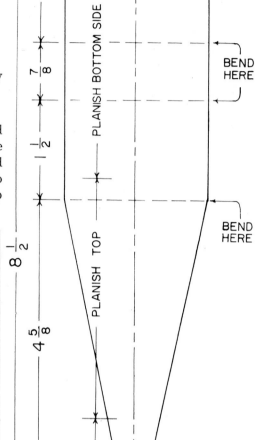

2. The holder metal is bent to shape over angle irons or, in school shops, in a brake. The scroll is formed over a small stake or round piece of steel.

3. The tray is soft soldered to the holder a little off center towards the holder as shown in the diagram.

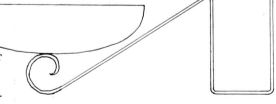

BEND TO THIS SHAPE

Fig. 165

MOUSE ASH TRAY

This interesting novelty ash tray is best made from copper.

MATERIAL   **soft coppper**

body	20 gauge	4¾″ x 6″
ring	18 gauge	¼″ x 5¼″
tail	18 gauge	3/16″ x 7″

PROCEDURE

1. Form pattern by folding paper in half—drawing ½ body—cutting with scissors—opening paper.
2. Trace body onto metal. Cut metal to shape with small curved shears and jeweler's saw. File.
3. Form body with silversmith hammer in hollow block (see fig. 66). Planish.
4. Planish head and ears.
5. Shape head as shown below.
6. Ears are domed slightly and then twisted to shape.
7. Band is silver soldered together, planished, and soft soldered to body.
8. Tail is planished, shaped, and soft soldered to body.

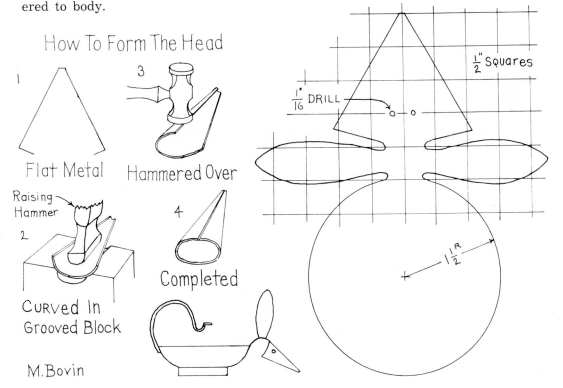

How To Form The Head

1 Flat Metal

3 Hammered Over

Raising Hammer

2 Curved In Grooved Block

4 Completed

M. Bovin

½″ Squares

1/16″ DRILL

1½ R

Fig. 166

CAULDRON ASH TRAY

Material: **Copper or Brass**

Tray: 18 gauge 3″ circle
Base: 18 gauge 2″ circle
Ring: 18 gauge 5/16 x 6″
Handle: 16 gauge ⅛″ x 4-1/8″
Support: 16 gauge ⅜″ x 7¼″
Holder: 18 gauge ½″ x ⅝″
Loop: 18 gauge 1/16″ x ¾″

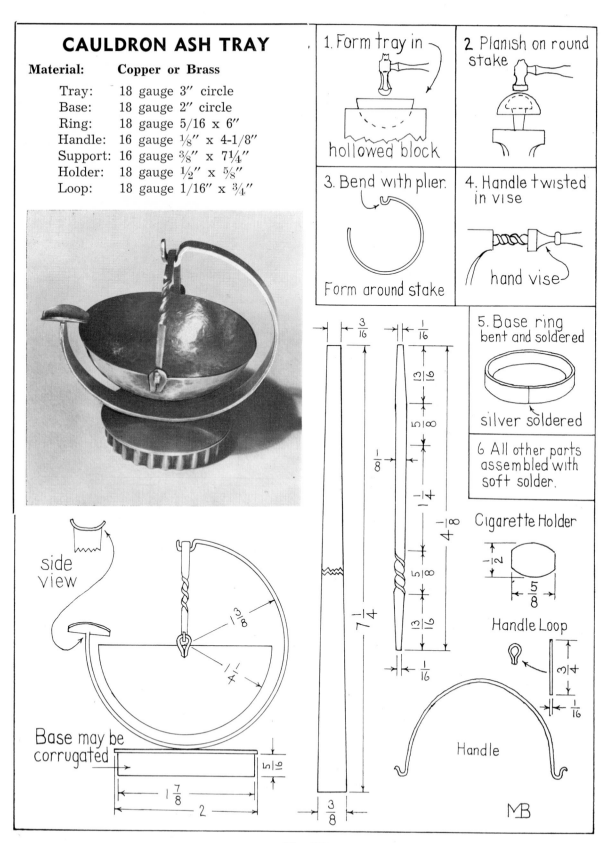

1. Form tray in hollowed block

2. Planish on round stake

3. Bend with plier. Form around stake

4. Handle twisted in vise — hand vise

5. Base ring bent and soldered — silver soldered

6. All other parts assembled with soft solder.

side view

Base may be corrugated

Cigarette Holder

Handle Loop

Handle

MB

Fig. 167

112

NOVELTY ASH CAN

Working Drawing

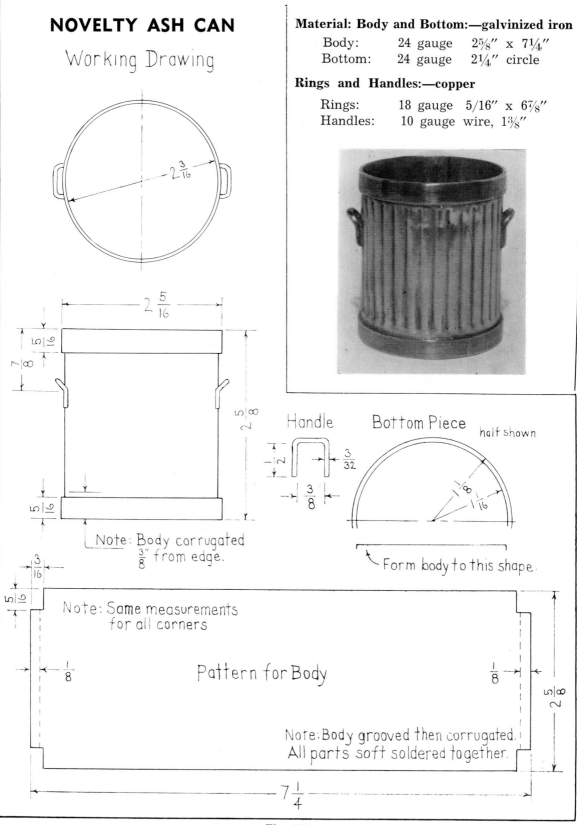

Material: Body and Bottom:—galvinized iron

Body: 24 gauge $2\frac{5}{8}''$ x $7\frac{1}{4}''$
Bottom: 24 gauge $2\frac{1}{4}''$ circle

Rings and Handles:—copper

Rings: 18 gauge   5/16'' x $6\frac{7}{8}''$
Handles: 10 gauge wire, $1\frac{3}{8}''$

$2\frac{3}{16}$

$2\frac{5}{16}$

$\frac{5}{16}$

$\frac{7}{8}$

$2\frac{5}{8}$

$\frac{5}{16}$

Note: Body corrugated $\frac{3}{8}''$ from edge.

Handle

2

$\frac{3}{32}$

$\frac{3}{8}$

Bottom Piece

half shown

$\frac{1}{8}$

$\frac{1}{16}$

Form body to this shape.

$\frac{3}{16}$

$\frac{5}{16}$

Note: Same measurements for all corners

$\frac{1}{8}$

Pattern for Body

$\frac{1}{8}$

$2\frac{5}{8}$

Note: Body grooved then corrugated.
All parts soft soldered together.

$7\frac{1}{4}$

Fig. 168

SMALL PICTURE FRAME

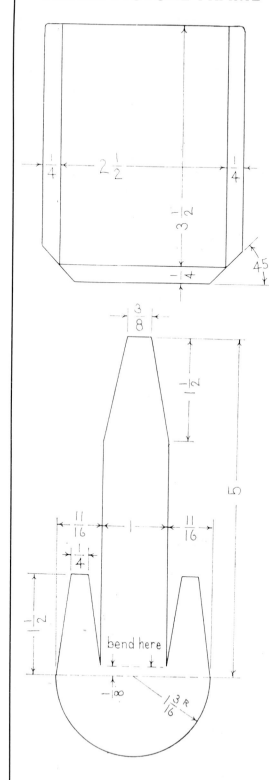

Material: 24 gauge half-hard copper
> 1 piece:—..3″ x 3¾″
> 1 piece:—2⅜″ x 6-3/16″

Note: If half-hard copper or brass are not available, soft copper or brass can be hardened by planishing lightly.

PROCEDURE: The metal is entirely cut to shape with hand shears.

The edges of the frame can be bent in over a 1/16″ piece of sheet metal. Where a brake is available, the frame can be formed as follows: Bend the bottom edge up to a 90° angle. Using the ends of the brake, bend the sides in as far as possible. Finally, hammer the bottom edge down over a 1/16″ piece of sheet metal until it meets the sides. If the metal overlaps where the bottom edge meets the side, cut through the edges with a fine jeweler's saw blade to form a perfect mitred edge.

The center part of the holder metal is bent in a vise to a 90° angle. With a round nose plier, the three ends of the holder are rolled in and down to hold the frame.

Fig. 169

SCROLL CANDLESTICKS

Material: **18 gauge copper**

Scrolls: 3″ x 12″
Holders: 1″ x 3″
Trays: 2¼″ circles
Rivets: ⅛″

Note: Scroll is planished and then the wide part is hammered to shape over a steel rod or small stake; the rest of the scroll is bent to shape by hand.

The scroll metal can be cut to shape with a hand shear or on a foot squaring shear.

The 1″ x 3″ holder metal is bent to form a tube and then silver soldered.

Tray and top of holder are crimped with narrow raising hammer.

All parts assembled with soft solder.

An antique finish is recommended for the scroll candlesticks.

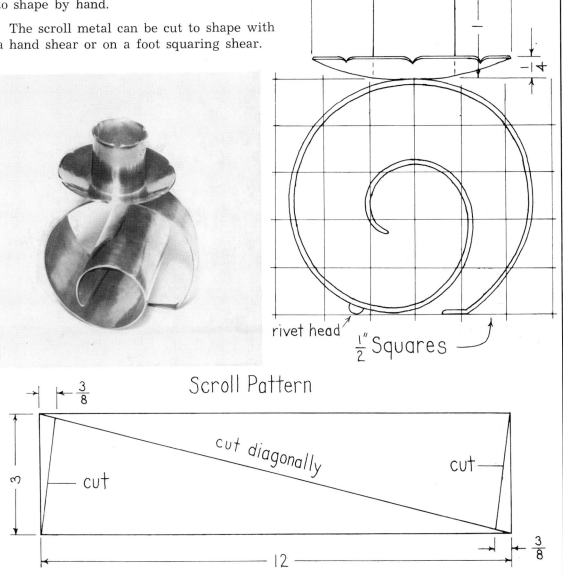

rivet head $\frac{1}{2}$″ Squares

Scroll Pattern

Fig. 170

SMALL WATERING CAN

Note: Silver solder body together. All other parts are to be assembled with soft solder.

Material: 22 gauge soft brass

Body:	2⅝″ x 7-7/16″
Bottom:	2½″ diameter disc.
Top:	2-7/16″ diameter disc
Handle:	¼″ tubing, 7″ long.
Spout:	5/16″ tubing, 6¼″ long

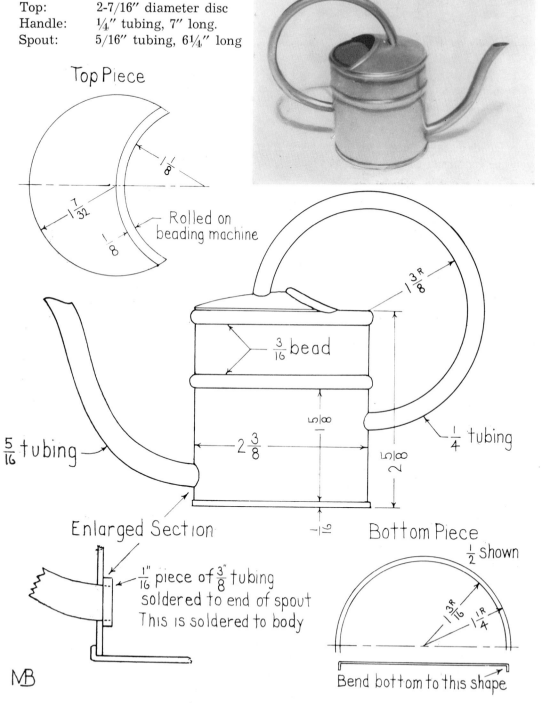

Top Piece

Rolled on beading machine

$\frac{3}{16}$ bead

$\frac{5}{16}$ tubing

$2\frac{3}{8}$

$\frac{1}{4}$ tubing

Enlarged Section

$\frac{1}{16}$″ piece of $\frac{3}{8}$″ tubing soldered to end of spout
This is soldered to body

Bottom Piece
$\frac{1}{2}$ shown

Bend bottom to this shape

MB

Fig. 171

BEER MUG

Material: **copper or brass**

    Body: 20 gauge, 4″ x 8″
    Band: 18 gauge, ¼″ x 8″
    Band: 18 gauge, ⅜″ x 8″
    Handle: 16 gauge, ¾″ x 5″
    Bottom: 20 gauge, 2-9/16″ circle

Note: Silver solder body metal to form tube and strips to form bands. Planish all metals and assemble with soft solder. Bands are stretched to fit body by planishing. Inside of the mug can be tinned and handle can be wrapped with lanyard or lacing.

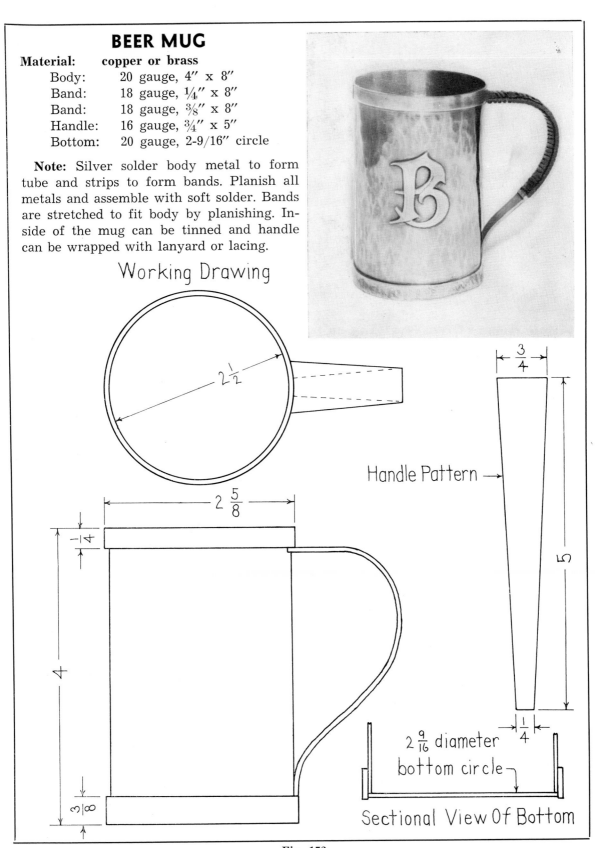

Working Drawing

Handle Pattern →

Sectional View Of Bottom

Fig. 172

WATERING CAN

MATERIAL: **20 gauge copper and brass**

Body	copper	5½" circle
Bottom	brass	4⅜" circle
Spout	brass	2" x 3½"
Rim	brass	⅜" x 4⅝"
Handle	brass	14 gauge, ¼" x 6¾"

PROCEDURE:

1. The body is formed by the beating down method—see page 50.

2. The opening for the rim is cut out with a jeweler's saw.

3. The edge of the bottom piece of metal is formed over a round bottom stake.

4. The seams of the spout and rim are silver soldered.

5. All parts are soft soldered to the body.

6. A group of 3/32" holes are drilled into the body where spout is soldered.

Handle   Spout

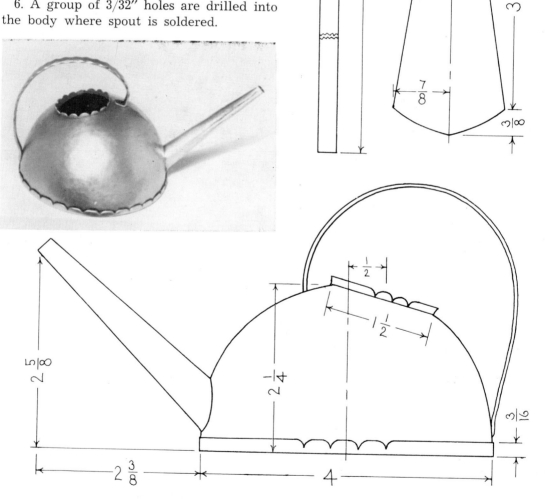

Fig. 173

CAT BOOK ENDS

Material: Copper or Brass, half-hard

Ends:	18 gauge, 3″ x 8½″
Cat:	16 gauge, 4½″ x 7″
Support:	⅛″ thick, 5/16″ x 1″

Note: Cat cut to shape with the jeweler's saw. Ends bent to shape shown in diagram for fish book ends. All parts assembled with soft solder. Planish soft copper or brass to harden if half-hard metal is not available.

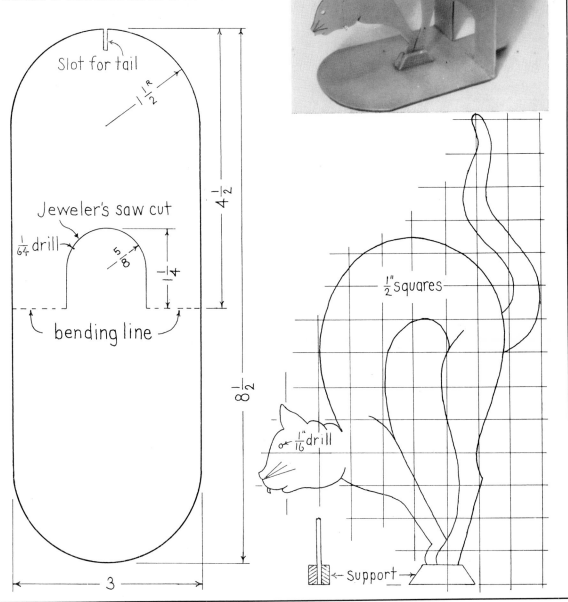

Slot for tail

$1\frac{1}{2}$ R

Jeweler's saw cut

$\frac{1}{64}$ drill

$\frac{5}{8}$

$\frac{1}{4}$

$4\frac{1}{2}$

bending line

$8\frac{1}{2}$

3

$\frac{1}{2}″$ squares

$\frac{1}{16}″$ drill

Support

Fig. 174

FISH BOOK ENDS

Material: Copper or Brass, half-hard

Ends: 18 gauge, 3″ x 10″
Fish: 16 gauge, 3″ x 4″

Note: Fish cut to shape with a jeweler's saw. Fish soldered to book ends with soft solder. Planish soft copper or brass to harden if half-hard metal is not available.

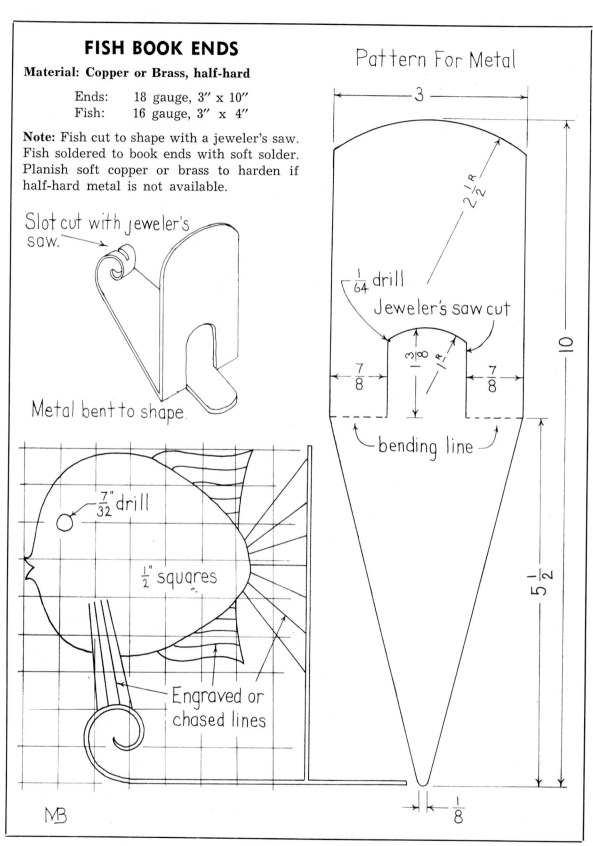

Slot cut with jeweler's saw.

Metal bent to shape.

Pattern For Metal

$2\frac{1}{2}$ R

$\frac{1}{64}$ drill

Jeweler's saw cut

$\frac{7}{8}$

$\frac{3}{8}$

$\frac{7}{8}$

1 R

bending line

3

10

$5\frac{1}{2}$

$\frac{1}{8}$

$\frac{7}{32}''$ drill

$\frac{1}{2}''$ squares

Engraved or chased lines

MB

Fig. 175

COWBOY HAT ASHTRAY

This novelty ash tray is recommended as an interesting and technically challenging craft project. Comparatively little material is required. Technically one receives training in development of a frustrum of a cone, forming of metal, filing, and hard and soft soldering.

MATERIAL: 20 gauge soft copper

    1 piece 4″ square
    1 piece 2″ x 5½″
    1 piece 1¾″ square
    18″ of 18 gauge brass wire

PROCEDURE

1. Develop frustrum of cone as shown in the diagram (2). Trace onto the copper, cut and bend to shape.
2. Cut 1⅝″ circle. Dome slightly. File and silver solder to crown.
3. With a raising hammer, hammer groove and hollows into the crown over a wood file handle which has been grooved to the required shape.
4. Cut and file 4″ circle for brim as shown in diagram 5. If desired, center can be removed with a jeweler's saw. Hammer to shape shown in the picture and planish.
5. Soft solder brim to crown. Weave band as shown in 7. If desired, twisted wires may be used. Silver solder band to form a ring. Fit to crown and then soft solder in position.

Fig. 176

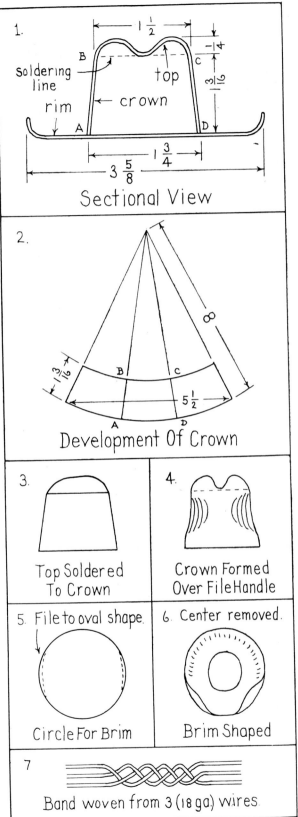

121

SILENT BUTLER

MATERIAL: copper or brass

Body:	20 gauge,	6¾″ circle
Cover:	20 gauge,	5½″ circle
Handle:	20 gauge,	1½″ x 5½″
Top:	18 gauge,	1⅛″ x 4½″
Opener:	16 gauge,	⅝″ x 1¼″
Tubing:	⅛″ diameter	

The body of the silent butler is straight raised as explained in figure 70. The cover is domed slightly and planished evenly. Note how the hollow handle is formed from two pieces of metal. The top of the handle is silver soldered to the bottom. The handle, after it has been filed and polished, is soft soldered to the body. The hinge and knob opener also are soft soldered.

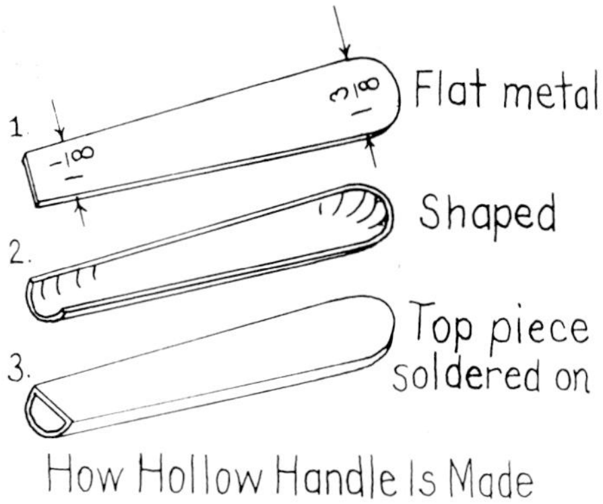

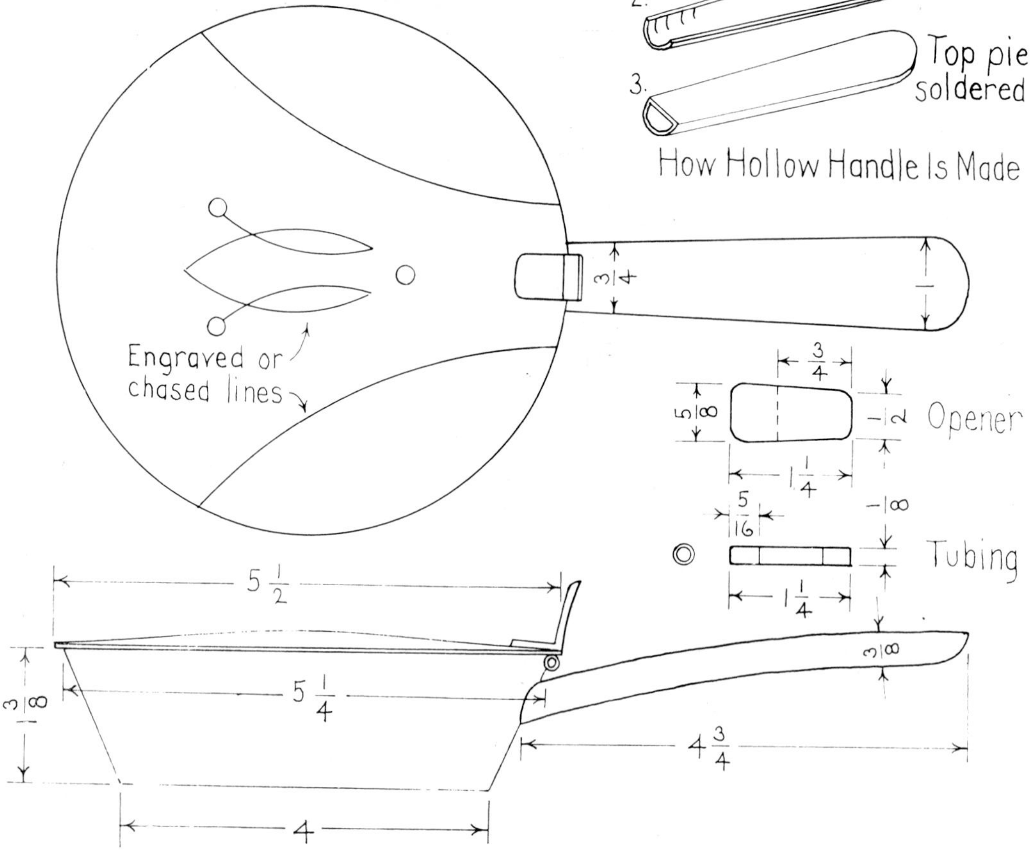

Fig. 177

COFFEE POT

This functional coffee pot is presented as an example of an object that can be designed and constructed by a beginning craftsman after a few of the fundamental techniques have been developed.

All parts of the coffee pot have been assembled with silver solder. If desired, the spout and support pieces are planished with a flat hammer and the hammer marks should be emeried and then polished off in order to give the object a contemporary straight line effect.

The body is developed as explained in figure 56 and the spout is made as explained in figure 127. The knob is held to the cover by means of two ½" #4 round head wood screws and the handle is held to the support pieces by means of #6 machine screws.

Note that the top and bottom pieces are cut slightly larger than required, planished, and after they have been soldered to the body their edges are trimmed with a small curved shear and filed flush with the body.

MATERIAL 20 gauge silver, copper, or brass wood handle and knob—ebony or mahogany

Body:	6¼" x 14"
Bottom:	3⅛" circle
Top:	5" circle
Spout:	2¾" x 4¼"
Top Ring:	¼" x 7¾"
Cover:	2¾" circle
Top Support:	¼" x ⅝" x 1⅛"
Bottom support:	¼" x ⅝" x 1⅛"

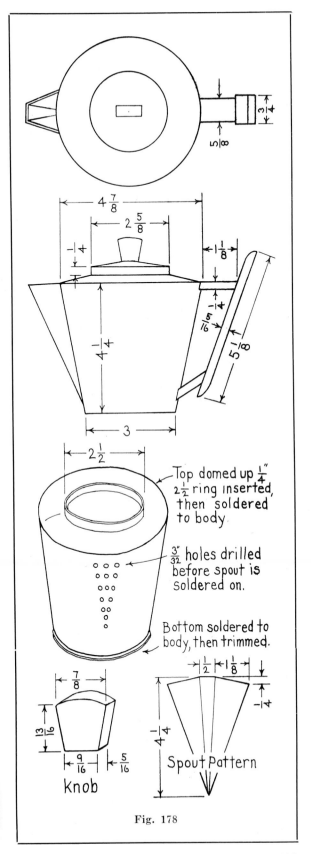

Top domed up ¼"
2½" ring inserted, then soldered to body.

3/32" holes drilled before spout is soldered on.

Bottom soldered to body, then trimmed.

knob

Spout Pattern

Fig. 178

SMALL TABLE LAMP

The dimensions of the lamp can be changed to fit individual needs. The edges of the shade were silver soldered together; they can be grooved. Picture on page 127.

Material:— **brass**

Center Tube:	7/16″ tubing, 10″ long
Leg:	1/4″ square, 15″ long
Shade:	24 gauge, 7 1/2″ x 10″
Back:	20 gauge, 1 1/2″ circle

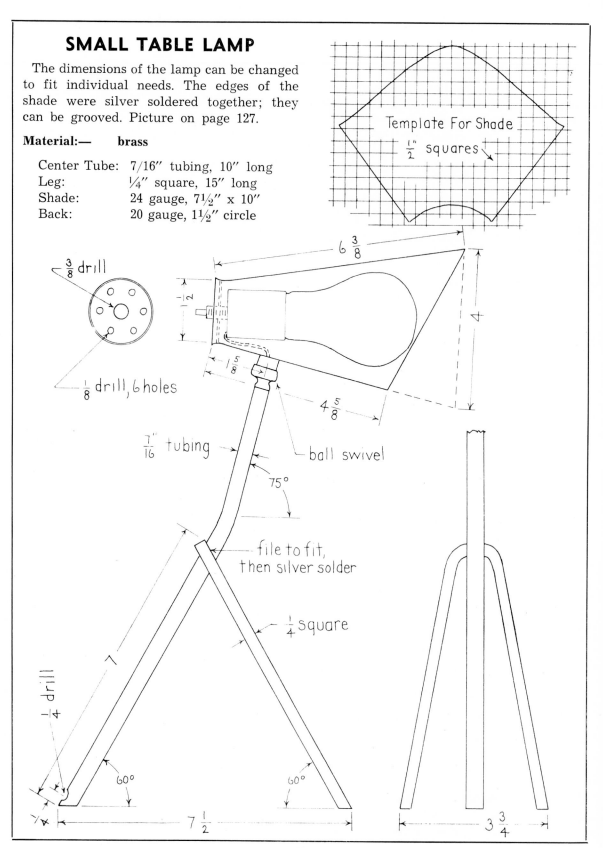

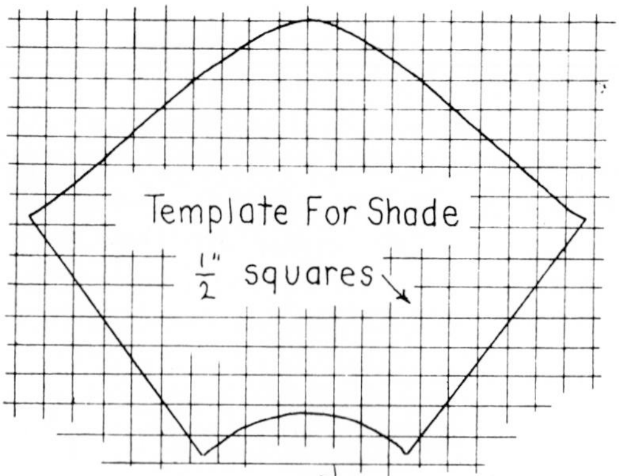
Template For Shade
1/2" squares

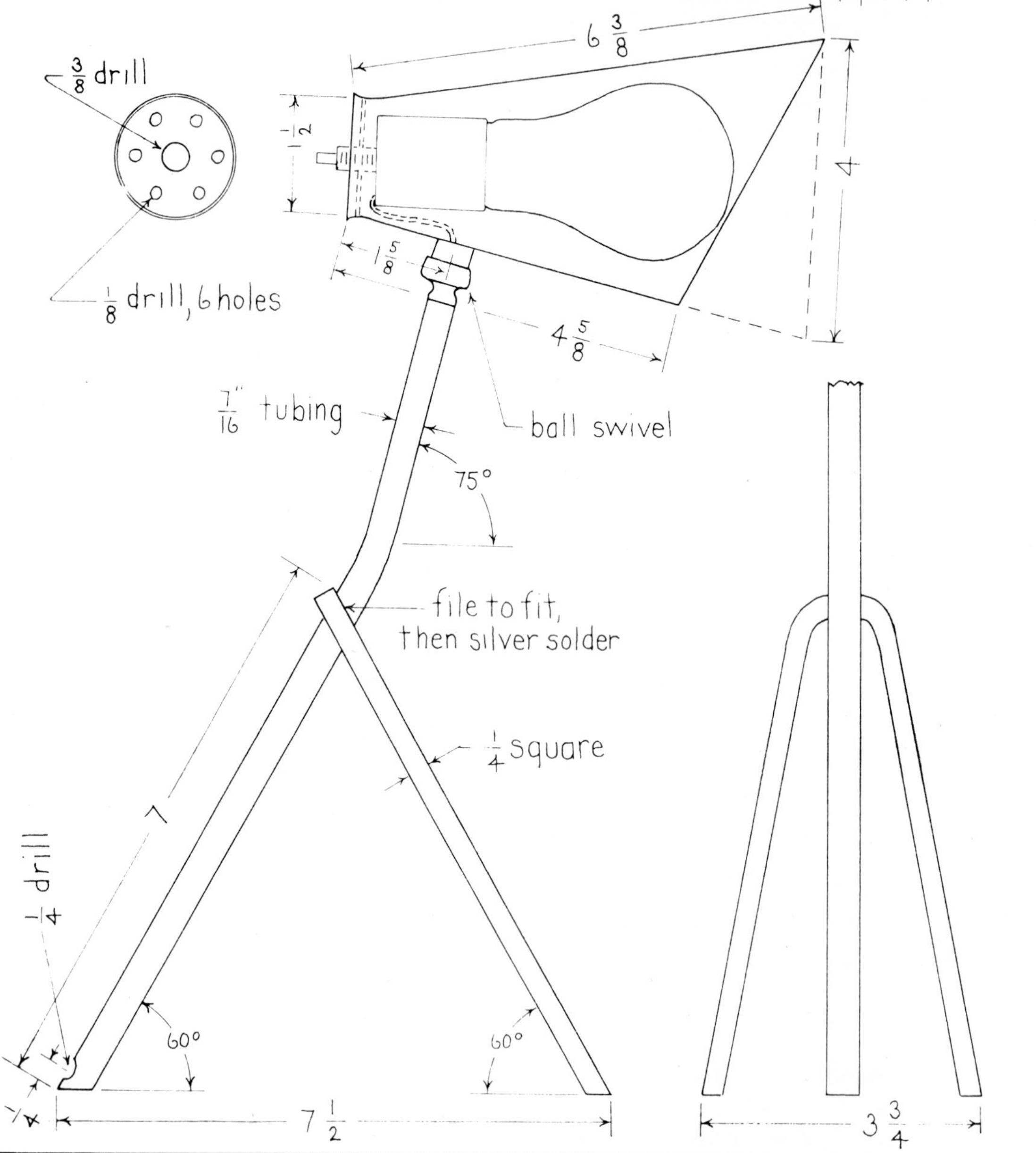
3/8 drill
1/8 drill, 6 holes
6 3/8
1 1/2
4
1 5/8
4 5/8
ball swivel
7/16" tubing
75°
file to fit, then silver solder
1/4 square
7
1/4 drill
60°
60°
1/4
7 1/2
3 3/4

Fig. 179

TORCH LAMP

Note: Rims, after being bent to rings, are silver soldered together. Legs are notched and soft soldered to bottom rim. Triangular bottom is soft soldered to legs. 18 gauge wire is used to staple plastic sheet to form shade. Shade is held in rims by means of rubber or duco cement. Picture on page 127.

Material: brass or copper

Top Rim:	22 gauge, 1/2" x 12"
Bottom Rim:	22 gauge, 5/8" x 12"
Bottom:	22 gauge, 3 1/4" triangle
3 Legs:	1/4" tubing, 1 1/4" long
plastic	7 5/8" x 12 1/4"

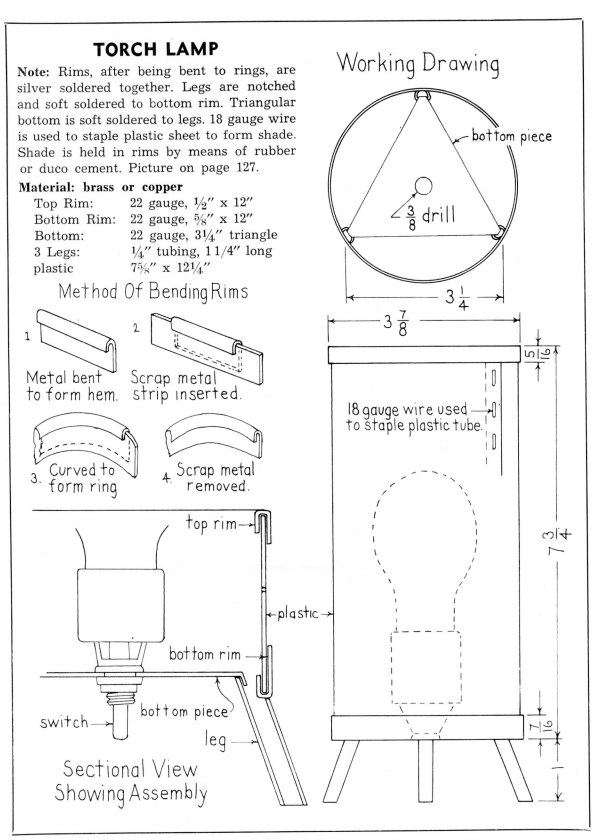

Method Of Bending Rims

1. Metal bent to form hem.
2. Scrap metal strip inserted.
3. Curved to form ring
4. Scrap metal removed.

Working Drawing

bottom piece

3/8 drill

3 1/4

3 7/8

5/16

18 gauge wire used to staple plastic tube.

7 3/4

7/16

Sectional View Showing Assembly

top rim

plastic

bottom rim

switch

bottom piece

leg

Fig. 180

125

LETTER OPENERS

The letter openers shown in figure 181 are design suggestions for school and camp programs and for beginning craftsmen. They were made from 14 and 16 gauge metal. 18 gauge can be used. The metal should be hard in order to retain its shape; soft metal can be hardened by planishing.

All letter openers were cut to shape with the jeweler's saw. Note that openers 4, 5, and 6 were designed so that the blade part could be cut on a foot squaring shear. The lines can be engraved or chased into the metal. The lines in number 2 opener were filled in with soft solder.

Where possible, soft solder parts to letter openers. When silver solder is used, planish the blade carefully to harden it.

The letter openers in figure 182 were handmade by craftsmen at The International Silver Company.

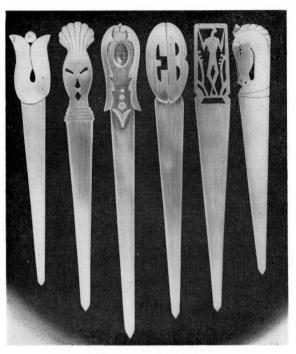

Fig. 181 Letter Openers

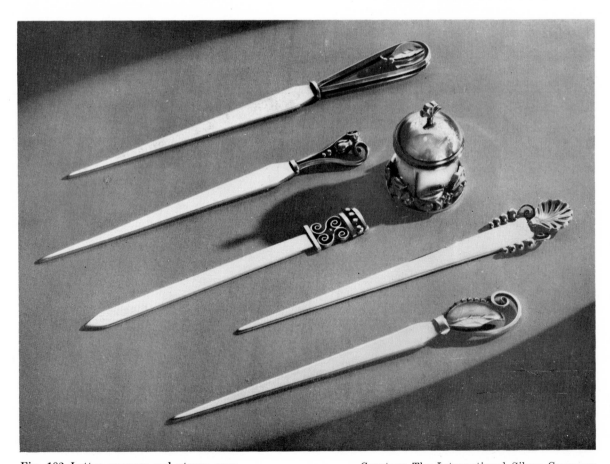

Fig. 182 Letter openers and stamp case

Courtesy The International Silver Company

Fig. 179A Small Table Lamp on page 124

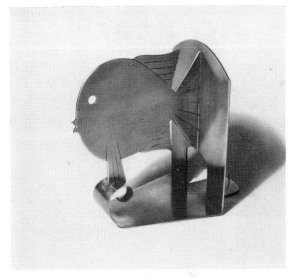

Fig. 175A Fish Book End on page 120

Fig. 183 Candlestick

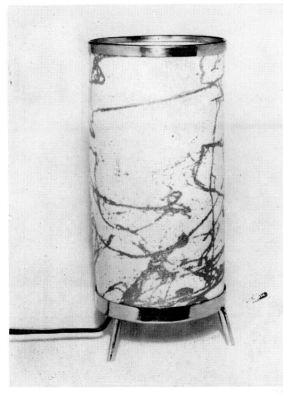

Fig. 180A Torch Lamp on page 125

Fig. 184 Novelty Box Ash Tray

REPRESENTATIVE OBJECTS
BY SILVERSMITHS

TUREEN
Paul Lamerie
English—1740's

BOWL
Cornelius Kiersteade
American—1740's

TANKARD
John Noyes
American—1720

COVERED BOWL
George Jensen
Danish 1930's

SILVER SERVICE
Wiener Werkstatte
German 1920's

1   **BOWL and LADLE**
    Hans Christianson
    Sterling Silver

2   **WATER PITCHER**
    Danish
    Sterling Silver

3   **WATER PITCHER**
    Hans Christianson
    Sterling Silver

1

2   3

4 **WATER PITCHER**
Frederick A. Miller
Sterling Silver

5 **WATER CRUET**
Kurt J. Matzdorf
Sterling Silver

6 **GRAVY BOWL and LADLE**
Herman Roth
Sterling Silver and Ebony

6

4   5

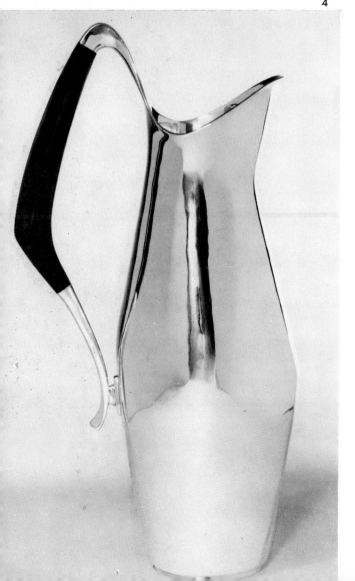

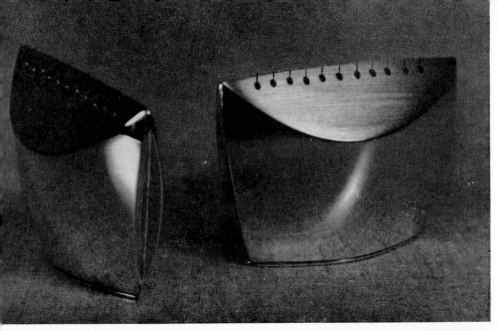

SALT and PEPPER
Silver
Al Pine

COFFEE SET
Silver and Rose Wood
Frederick Lauritzen

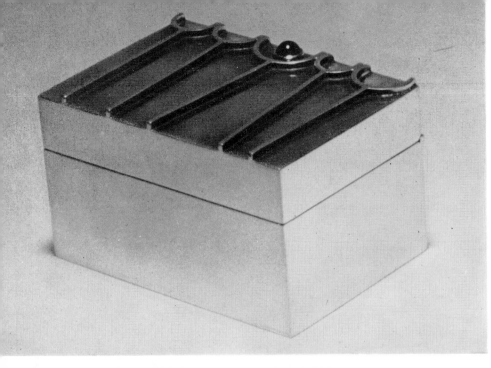

SILVER BOX
Frederick Lauritzen

COFFEE SET
Silver and Ebony
Herman Roth

CIGARETTE BOX
Sterling Silver

MARTINI PITCHER
Silver and Rosewood
Kurt Matzdorf

CANDY DISH
Sterling Silver

CANDELABRAS
Silver and Ebony
Frederick A. Miller

BLACK ONYX NODE   Harold Schremmer

EBONY NODE   Harold Milbrat

SILVER CHALICES

14K GOLD EMBLEMS   Olaf Skoogfors

CHASED NODE   William Seit

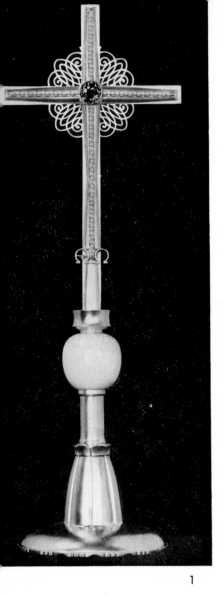

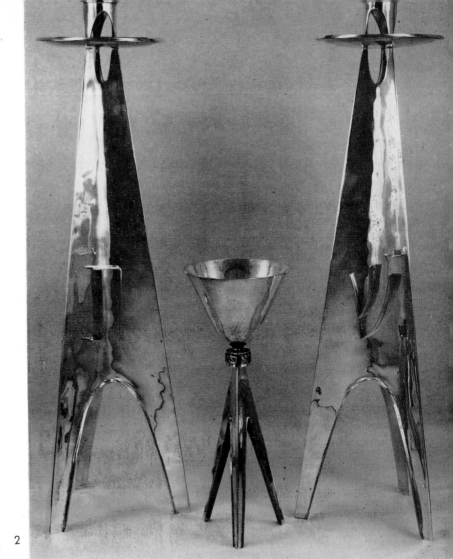

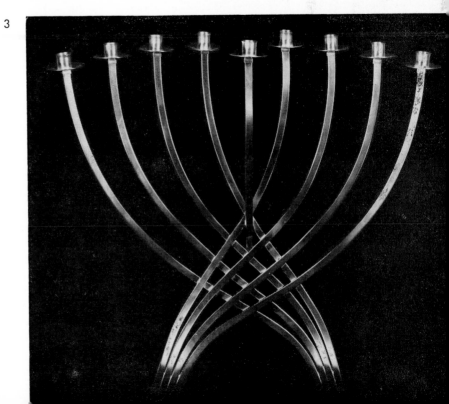

1

2

3

1 **ALTAR CROSS**
Carl Podszus

2 **CANDLE HOLDERS
and KIDDUSH CUP**
Ludwig Wolpert

3 **MENORAH**
Ludwig Wolpert

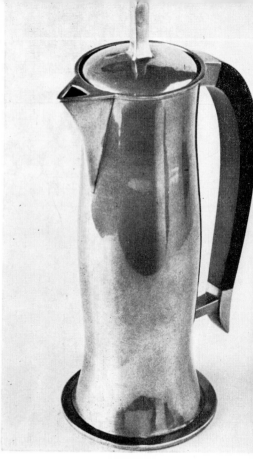

COFFEE POT — C. Richmond, II

COFFEE POT — Walter Rhodes

VASE — Frederick A. Miller

WATER PITCHER — Frederick A. Miller

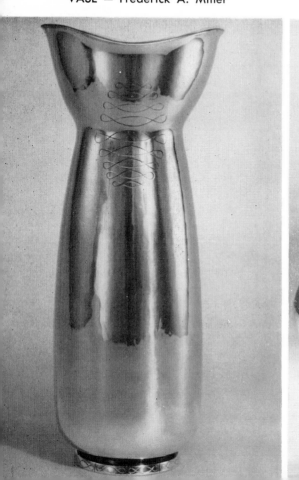

COFFEE POT   Fred Fenster

TEAPOT ON STAND   Fred Fenster

TEA KETTLE   Fred Fenster

CANDELABRA   Bernard Bernstein

PITCHER   Danish

WATER JUG   Karl Hansen

STERLING SILVERSMITHS GUILD OF AMERICA
Student Design Award Winners

COFFEE SERVICE   Edward Trelan, 1960

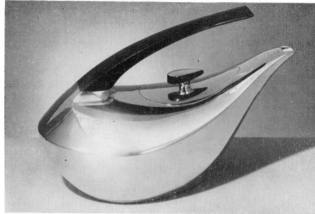

TEAPOT   Michael P. Ribar, 1961

CANDY DISH   Mark Kelly, 1962

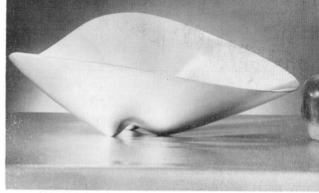

FRUIT BOWL   Stephen Parish, 1960

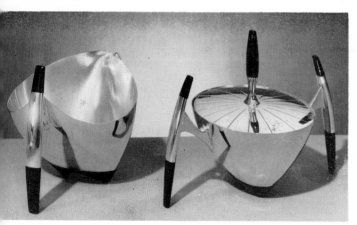

CREAM AND SUGAR SET   Daniel Buckley, 1961

CREAM AND SUGAR SET   Jack Pink, 1960

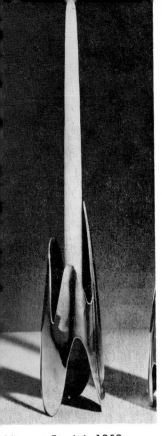

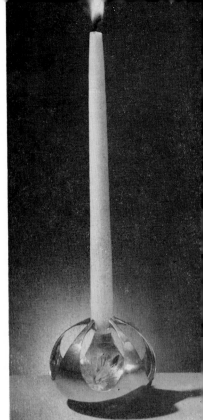

Vincent Ferrini, 1959   Pitcher — Condon Kuhl, 1963   C. R. Helms, 1961

Goblet — Lynda R. Ames, 1960   Vase — Johan Schumm, 1961

APPENDIX

Troy Weight

24 grains .... 1 pennyweight
20 pennyweights .... 1 ounce
12 ounces .... 1 pound

The troy ounce is about 10% heavier than the commonly used avoirdupois ounce.

Avoirdupois ounces x 0.9115 = troy ounces.

Avoirdupois Weight

27-1/3 grains .... 1 dram
16 drams .... 1 ounce
16 ounces .... 1 pound

The avoirdupois pound is about 21½% heavier than the troy pound.

Troy ounces x 1.0971 = avoirdupois ounces.

Weight Relationships

1 gram .... 15.432 grains
1 oz. avoird. .... 28.25 grains
1 oz. troy .... 31.10 grams

1 carat .... 3.086 grains
1 lb. avoird. .... 7000 grains
1 lb. troy .... 5760 grains

Comparative Weights of Equal Volumes

Coin Silver is .... .995 " " " " Aluminum
Sterling Silver is .... .998 " " " " Sterling Silver
.796 " " " " Aluminum
1.163 " " " " Sterling Silver
3.852 " " " " Sterling Silver
Copper is .... .895 times as heavy as Fine Silver
3.311 " " " " Fine Silver
14 K Yellow Gold is .... 1.257 " " " " 14 K. Yellow Gold
Platinum is .... 2.063 " " " " Copper

Specific Gravity, Melting Point, and Weight of Meal and Alloys

Metal	Melting Point °F.	Melting Point °C.	Specific Gravity	Weight in Troy ozs. per cu. in.	Metal	Melting Point °F.	Melting Point °C.	Specific Gravity	Weight in Troy ozs. per cu. in.
Aluminum	1220	660	2.70	1.423	Iridium	4449	2454	22.40	11.802
Antimony	1167	630	6.62	3.488	Iron (pure)	2795	1535	7.86	4.141
Beryllium	2462	1350	1.82	.959	Lead	621	327	11.36	5.985
Bismuth	520	271	9.80	5.163	Magnesium	1204	651	1.74	917
Cadmium	610	321	8.67	4.568	Manganese	2273	1245	7.2	3.793
Carbon	.....	.....	2.22	1.170	Molybdenum	4748	2620	10.20	5.374
Chromium	3326	1830	7.14	3.762	Nickel	2645	1452	8.85	4.663
Cobalt	2696	1480	8.90	4.689	Osmium	4892	2700	22.48	11.844
Copper	1981	1083	8.94	4.710	Palladium	2831	1555	12.00	6.322
Gold	1945	1063	19.36	10.200	Phosphorus	111	44	1.82	.959
18 Kt. green	1810	988	15.90	8.375	Platinum	3224	1773	21.45	11.301
18 Kt. yellow	1700	927	15.58	8.211	15% Iridio Plat.	3310	1821	21.59	11.373
18 Kt. white	1730	943	14.64	7.712	10% Iridio Plat.	3250	1788	21.54	11.349
18 Kt. red	1655	902	15.18	7.998	5% Iridio Plat.	3235	1779	21.50	11.325
14 Kt. green	1765	963	14.20	7.482	Rhodium	3551	1955	12.5	6.586
14 Kt. yellow	1615	879	13.07	6.885	Ruthenium	4442	2450	12.2	6.428
14 Kt. white	1825	996	12.61	6.642	Silicon	2588	1420	2.40	1.264
14 Kt. red	1715	935	13.26	6.986	Silver	1761	961	10.53	5.548
10 Kt. green	1580	860	11.03	5.810	Sterling	1640	893	10.40	5.477
10 Kt. yellow	1665	907	11.57	6.096	Coin	1615	879	10.35	5.451
10 Kt. white	1975	1079	11.07	5.832	Tin	450	232	7.30	3.846
10 Kt. red	1760	960	11.59	6.106	Zinc	787	419	7.14	3.762

SHEET METAL

Weight Per Square Inch by B & S Gauge

B & S Gauge	Thickness in Inches	Fine Silver Ozs.	Sterling Silver Ozs.	Coin Silver Ozs.	Fine Gold Dwts.	10K Yel. Gold Dwts.	14K Yel. Gold Dwts.	18K Yel. Gold Dwts.	Platinum Ozs.	Palladium Ozs.
1	28930	1 61	1 58	1 58	59 0	35.3	39.8	47.5	3.27	1.83
2	25763	1 43	1 41	1 40	52 6	31.4	35.5	42.3	2.91	1.63
3	22942	1 27	1 26	1.25	46.8	28.0	31.6	37.7	2.59	1.45
4	20431	1 13	1 12	1 11	41 7	24.9	28.1	33.6	2.31	1.29
5	18194	1 01	996	992	37.1	22.2	25.1	29.9	2.06	1.15
6	16202	899	887	883	33.1	19.8	22.3	26.6	1.83	1.02
7	14428	800	.790	.786	29.4	17.6	19.9	23.7	1.63	.912
8	12849	713	704	.700	26 2	15.7	17.7	21.1	1.45	.812
9	11443	635	627	624	23.3	14.0	15 8	18.8	1.29	.723
10	10189	565	558	.555	20.8	12 4	14.0	16.7	1.15	.644
11	09074	503	.497	495	18 5	11 1	12.5	14 9	1.03	574
12	08080	.448	443	440	16.5	9.85	11.1	13.3	.913	511
13	.07196	399	.394	.392	14 7	8.77	9 91	11.8	813	.455
14	06408	356	351	349	13.1	7 81	8.82	10.5	.724	405
15	05706	317	313	311	11.6	6.96	7.86	9 37	.645	361
16	05082	.282	278	277	10.4	6.21	7.00	8.35	574	321
17	04525	.251	.248	.247	9.23	5.52	6.23	7 43	511	286
18	04030	.224	.221	.220	8.22	4.91	5.55	6 62	455	255
19	03589	.199	.197	196	7.32	4.38	4.94	5.89	406	227
20	03196	.177	175	.174	6 52	3.90	4.40	5 25	361	202
21	02846	158	.156	.155	5.81	3.47	3.92	4 67	322	180
22	.02534	141	.139	.138	5.17	3.09	3 49	4 16	286	160
23	.02257	.125	.124	.123	4.60	2.75	3.11	3 71	255	143
24	.02010	.112	.110	110	4.10	2.45	2.77	3.30	.227	127
25	.01790	.0993	.0980	.0976	3.65	2.18	2.46	2.94	202	113
26	.01594	.0884	.0873	.0869	3.25	1.94	2.19	2.62	.180	.101
27	01419	.0787	.0777	.0773	2.89	1.73	1.95	2 33	160	.0897
28	.01264	.0701	.0692	.0689	2.58	1.54	1.74	2.08	.143	0799
29	.01125	.0624	.0616	.0613	2.29	1.37	1.55	1 85	.127	0711
30	.01002	0556	.0549	.0546	2.04	1.22	1.38	1.65	.113	.0633
31	.00892	0495	.0489	.0486	1.82	1.09	1.23	1.46	.101	.0564
32	.00795	.0441	.0435	.0433	1.62	.969	1.09	1.31	.0898	0503
33	00708	0393	0388	.0386	1.44	.863	.975	1.16	.0800	.0448
34	00630	.0350	0345	.0343	1.29	.768	.868	1.03	.0712	.0398
35	00561	.0311	0307	.0306	1.14	.684	.772	.921	.0634	.0355
36	.00500	0277	.0274	.0273	1.02	.610	.689	.821	.0565	.0316
37	.00445	.0247	.0244	.0243	.908	.543	.613	.731	.0503	0281
38	00396	0220	0217	.0216	.808	.483	.545	.650	0448	.0250
39	00353	.0196	.0193	.0192	.720	.430	.486	.580	.0399	0223
40	00314	.0174	.0172	.0171	.641	383	.432	.516	.0355	.0199

ROUND WIRE

Weight in Pennyweights or Ounces Per Foot in B & S Gauge

B & S Gauge	Thick-ness in Inches	Fine Silver Ozs.	Sterling Silver Ozs.	Coin Silver Ozs.	Fine Gold Dwts.	10K Yel. Gold Dwts.	14K Yel. Gold Dwts.	18K Yel. Gold Dwts.	Plat-inum Ozs.	Palla-dium Ozs.
1	.28930	4 38	4 32	4.30	161.0	96.2	109.	130.	8.91	4.99
2	.25763	3 47	3 43	3.41	128.	76.3	86.1	104.	7.07	3.94
3	.22942	2 75	2.72	2 70	101.	60.5	68.3	81.5	5.61	3.19
4	.20431	2.18	2 15	2.14	80.3	48.0	54.2	64.6	4.45	2.42
5	18194	1 73	1 71	1 70	63 6	38.0	43.0	51.2	3.53	1.97
6	.16202	1 37	1 36	1 35	50.5	30.2	34.1	40 6	2.80	1.56
7	.14428	1 09	1 07	1 07	40.0	23.9	27.0	32.2	2.22	1.24
8	.12849	863	.852	.848	31.7	19.0	21.4	25.6	1.76	.984
9	.11443	685	.676	.673	25.2	15.1	17.0	20 3	1.39	.780
10	10189	.543	.536	.533	20.0	11.9	13.5	16.1	1.11	.619
11	.09074	.431	425	423	15.8	9.46	10.7	12.7	.877	.491
12	.08080	.341	337	.335	12.6	7.50	8.47	10.1	.695	.389
13	07196	.271	.267	.266	9.96	5.95	6.72	8.01	.552	.309
14	.06408	.215	.212	.211	7.89	4.72	5.33	6.36	.437	.495
15	.05706	.170	.168	.167	6 26	3.74	4.23	5.04	.347	154
16	.05082	.135	.133	.133	4.97	2.97	3.35	4.00	.275	.154
17	04525	.107	.106	.105	3.94	2.35	2.66	3.17	.218	.122
18	.04030	.0849	0838	.0834	3.12	1.87	2.11	2.51	.173	.0968
19	.03589	.0674	.0665	.0662	2.48	1.48	1.67	1.99	.137	.0767
20	.03196	0534	.0527	.0525	1 96	1.17	1.33	1.58	.109	.0609
21	.02846	.0424	.0418	.0416	1.56	.931	1.05	1.25	0863	.0483
22	.02534	.0336	.0331	.0330	1.23	.738	.833	.994	.0684	.0383
23	.02257	.0266	.0263	.0262	.979	.585	.661	.789	.0543	.0304
24	.02010	.0211	.0209	.0203	.777	.464	.524	.625	.0430	.0241
25	.01790	.0168	.0165	.0165	.616	.368	.416	.496	.0341	.0191
26	.01594	.0133	.0131	.0131	.489	.292	.330	.393	.0271	.0151
27	.01419	.0105	.0104	.0103	.387	.231	.261	.312	.0214	.0120
28	.01264	.00835	.00825	.00821	.307	.184	.207	.247	.0170	.00952
29	.01125	.00662	.00653	.00650	.243	.145	.164	.196	.0135	.00754
30	.01002	.00525	.00518	.00516	.193	.115	.130	.155	.0107	.00598
81	.00892	.00416	.00411	.00409	.153	.0914	.103	.123	.00847	.00474
32	.00795	.00330	.00326	.00325	.122	.0726	.0820	.0973	.00673	.00377
33	.00708	.00262	.00259	.00258	.0964	.0576	.0651	.0776	.00534	.00299
34	.00630	.00208	.00205	.00204	.0763	.0456	.0515	.0614	.00423	.00286
35	.00561	.00165	.00162	.00162	.0605	.0362	.0408	.0487	.00335	.00188
36	.00500	.00131	.00129	.00128	.0481	.0287	.0324	.0387	.00266	.00149
37	.00445	.00104	.00102	.00102	.0381	.0228	.0257	.0306	.00211	.00118
38	.00396	.000820	.000809	.000806	.0302	.0180	.0204	.0243	.00167	.000934
39	.00353	.000652	.000643	.000640	.0240	.0143	.0162	.0193	.00133	.000742
40	.00314	.000516	.000509	.000507	.0190	.0113	.0128	.0153	.00105	.000587

Square Wire is 1.27324 times as heavy as round wire of the same gauge.

STERLING CIRCLES
Weight in Ounces for Various Diameters in B & S Gauge

Dia. in Inches	B & S GAUGE											
	15	16	17	18	19	20	21	22	23	24	25	26
¼	.0153	.0137	.0122	.0108	.0097	.0086	.0077	.0068	.0061	.0054	.0048	.0043
½	.0614	.0547	.0487	.0433	.0386	.0344	.0306	.0273	.0243	.0216	.0193	.0171
¾	.138	.123	.109	.0975	.0868	.0773	.0689	.0613	.0546	.0486	.0433	.0386
1	.245	.219	.195	.173	.154	.137	.122	.109	.0971	.0865	.0770	.0686
1¼	.384	.342	.304	.271	.241	.215	.191	.170	.152	.135	.120	.107
1½	.552	.492	.438	.390	.347	.309	.275	.245	.218	.195	.173	.154
1¾	.752	.669	.596	.531	.473	.421	.375	.334	.297	.265	.236	.210
2	.982	.874	.779	.693	.618	.550	.490	.436	.388	.346	.308	.274
2¼	1.24	1.11	.985	.878	.782	.696	.620	.552	.492	.438	.390	.347
2½	1.53	1.37	1.22	1.08	.965	.859	.765	.681	.607	.540	.481	.429
2¾	1.86	1.65	1.47	1.31	1.17	1.04	.926	.824	.734	.654	.582	.519
3	2.21	1.97	1.75	1.56	1.39	1.24	1.10	.981	.874	.778	.693	.617
3¼	2.59	2.31	2.06	1.83	1.63	1.45	1.29	1.15	1.03	.913	.813	.724
3½	3.01	2.68	2.38	2.12	1.89	1.68	1.50	1.34	1.19	1.06	.943	.840
3¾	3.45	3.07	2.74	2.44	2.17	1.93	1.72	1.53	1.37	1.22	1.08	.964
4	3.93	3.50	3.11	2.77	2.47	2.20	1.96	1.74	1.55	1.38	1.23	1.10
4¼	4.43	3.95	3.52	3.13	2.79	2.48	2.21	1.97	1.75	1.56	1.39	1.24
4½	4.97	4.43	3.94	3.51	3.13	2.78	2.48	2.21	1.97	1.75	1.56	1.39
4¾	5.54	4.93	4.39	3.91	3.48	3.10	2.76	2.46	2.19	1.95	1.74	1.55
5	6.14	5.47	4.87	4.33	3.86	3.44	3.06	2.73	2.43	2.16	1.93	1.71
5¼	6.77	6.03	5.37	4.78	4.26	3.79	3.37	3.00	2.68	2.38	2.12	1.89
5½	7.43	6.61	5.89	5.24	4.67	4.16	3.70	3.30	2.94	2.62	2.33	2.07
5¾	8.12	7.23	6.44	5.73	5.10	4.55	4.05	3.60	3.21	2.86	2.55	2.27
6	8.84	7.87	7.01	6.24	5.56	4.95	4.41	3.92	3.50	3.11	2.77	2.47
6¼	9.59	8.54	7.60	6.77	6.03	5.37	4.78	4.26	3.79	3.38	3.01	2.68
6½	10.4	9.24	8.22	7.32	6.52	5.81	5.17	4.61	4.10	3.65	3.25	2.90
6¾	11.2	9.96	8.87	7.90	7.03	6.26	5.58	4.97	4.42	3.94	3.51	3.12
7	12.0	10.7	9.54	8.49	7.56	6.74	6.00	5.34	4.76	4.24	3.77	3.36
7¼	12.9	11.5	10.2	9.11	8.11	7.23	6.43	5.73	5.10	4.54	4.05	3.60
7½	13.8	12.3	10.9	9.75	8.68	7.73	6.89	6.13	5.46	4.86	4.33	3.86
7¾	14.7	13.1	11.7	10.4	9.27	8.26	7.35	6.55	5.83	5.19	4.62	4.12
8	15.7	14.0	12.5	11.1	9.88	8.80	7.84	6.98	6.21	5.53	4.93	4.39
8¼	16.7	14.9	13.2	11.8	10.5	9.36	8.33	7.42	6.61	5.88	5.24	4.67
8½	17.7	15.8	14.1	12.5	11.2	9.93	8.85	7.88	7.01	6.25	5.56	4.95
8¾	18.8	16.7	14.9	13.3	11.8	10.5	9.37	8.35	7.43	6.62	5.90	5.25
9	19.9	17.7	15.8	14.0	12.5	11.1	9.92	8.83	7.86	7.00	6.24	5.55
9¼	21.0	18.7	16.7	14.8	13.2	11.8	10.5	9.33	8.31	7.40	6.59	5.87
9½	22.0	19.7	17.6	15.6	13.9	12.4	11.0	9.84	8.76	7.80	6.95	6.19
9¾	23.3	20.8	18.5	16.5	14.7	13.1	11.6	10.4	9.23	8.22	7.32	6.52
10	24.5	21.9	19.5	17.3	15.4	13.7	12.2	10.9	9.71	8.65	7.70	6.86

Courtesy of Handy & Harman

USEFUL INFORMATION

HANDMADE The term handmade can only be applied to jewelry objects made entirely by hand without the use of machine tools.

FINE SILVER is commercially pure silver—contains no alloy material.

COMMERCIAL SILVER is a term applied to silver that is 999 fine or higher.

STERLING SILVER is 925/1000 ($92\frac{1}{2}\%$) fine silver and 75/1000 ($7\frac{1}{2}\%$) copper. This proportion is fixed by law.

COIN SILVER is 900/1000 (90%) fine silver and the balance copper. The same alloy is used for U.S. silver coins.

FOREIGN SILVERWARE contains varying percentages of silver. In some cases the fineness is as low as 700/1000.

DANISH SILVER Silverware made in Denmark is 830/1000 fine silver if made to minimum Danish standards. 925/1000 fine silver is made for export.

SILVER PLATED WARE is made by electroplating fine silver on a base metal alloy —usually nickel silver or Britannia metal, sometimes brass or copper. This inexpensive process was perfected for industrial purposes around 1840.

SHEFFIELD PLATE (originally) was made by bonding sheet silver to copper, rolling and manufacturing into hollow-ware. The original process was abandoned about 1840 due to the introduction of electroplating. Imitations are made by electroplating silver on copper and are sometimes erroneously advertised as sheffield plate.

NICKEL SILVER—so-called—is a composition of nickel, copper and zinc. (It contains **no** silver).

GERMAN SILVER—a misleading name—the same as nickel silver. (It contains **no** silver).

BRITANNIA METAL is a composition of tin, copper and antimony.

PEWTER (original) was primarily a tin-lead alloy. It is now made in a tin, copper, antimony composition similar to Britannia metal.

HIGH BRASSES run from 55% copper in the extruded brass to 70% copper in the deep drawing brass—the balance being zinc.

LOW BRASSES contain 80% or more copper, the balance being zinc.

A PENNYWEIGHT is the twentieth part of a troy ounce. The name originally applied to the weight of an Anglo-Norman penny.

AN OUNCE (troy) is about 10% heavier than the common avoirdupois ounce. There are 14.583 ounces troy in an avoirdupois pound.

146

KARAT is a measure of fineness—24 karat is fine gold. One karat equals 1/24 (.0417). Thus 14 karat gold is 14/24 fine gold and the balance (10/24) alloy. If the gold content of an object is less than 10/24 the object can not be represented as karat gold.

CARAT is a unit of weight. One carat equals 3.086 grains or 1/5 of a gram. The diamond carat is subdivided into 100 parts or points. Thus, a fifty point diamond equals ½ of a carat and a 25 point diamond equals ¼ of a carat.

UNITED STATES STAMPING LAWS
Concerning Gold, Silver and Their Alloys
SUMMARY OF THE MAIN PROVISIONS

GOLD If an article is made of gold and is stamped gold, it must also bear a quality mark such as "10 karat" (10-K), "14 karat" (14-K).

If an article of gold is given a quality mark, the fineness by assay must not be lower than:—

Watch Cases and Flatware . . . . .003 less than stamped quality.
Other articles, not including solder . . . . .0208 (½ karat) less than the stamped quality.

However, the assay of a complete article, including solder, must not be more than .0417 (1 karat) under the stamped fineness per karat. **For example,** the gold in a 14-karat watch case, free from solder must be at least .5803 by assay. The entire case, including solder, must assay at least .547 (13 karat). A gold ring, not soldered, stamped "14-K" must assay at least .5625 (13½ karat.) The gold in a brooch stamped "10-K" must assay at least .3958 (9½ karat) and the entire brooch, solder and all, must assay at least .3750 (9 karat).

SILVER The silver in any article stamped "Sterling Silver" should assay .925, and the silver in an article marked "Coin Silver" should assay .900. The silver in an article, not including solder, must not be less than .004. **For example,** an article marked "Sterling Silver" free from solder, must assay at least .921.

Soldered parts must not reduce the assay of the entire article, including solder, by more than .010 under the standard assays of .925 and .900, respectively, for sterling silver and coin silver. For example, an article marked sterling silver when melted, including solder, must assay at least .915.

GOLD AND SILVER USED WITH INFERIOR METALS. An article made of an inferior base metal combined with gold may be marked "Rolled Gold Plate," "Gold Plate," "Gold Electroplate" or "Gold Filled" as the case may be. If any mark is used to indicate the fitness of the gold, it must be accompanied by one of these terms. **For example:—** "10 K. Rolled Gold Plate," "14 K Gold Filled."

The words "Sterling" or "Coin" alone or in combination with other metals cannot be used to describe a plated article. **For example:—**"Sterling Plate" is prohibited.

AN AMENDMENT TO THE STAMPING LAWS. Effective July 1, 1962. All articles which are stamped, tagged or labeled to indicate gold or silver content must also bear the trademark or name of a domestic (U.S.) concern.

The purpose of the amendment is to identify clearly a domestic firm responsible for the quality of a finished product bearing a gold or silver quality mark.

Imported gold or silver articles also must carry the mark or name of the importer, retailer or other firm or person who will be responsible for the quality of the article.

PENALTIES Violators may be fined up to $500 or be imprisoned up to three months, or both, at the discretion of the court.

SOURCES OF SUPPLY It is advisable to consult local classified telephone directories for local supply houses. The dealers listed below alphabetically by state and city, all stated that they sell to schools, tradesmen and craftsmen.

JEWELRY TOOLS AND FINDINGS

F. T. Skelton Co., Inc.
201 Frank Nelson Blvd.
Birmingham, Ala.

Paul's Inc.
113 Bill Street
Montgomery, Ala.

Langert Bros.
326 Goodrich Bldg.
Phoenix, Ariz.

Phoenix Jewelers Supplies
27 West Roosevelt
Phoenix, Arizona

American Handicraft Co.
2429 W. Manchester Blvd.
Inglewood, Calif.

American Handicraft Co.
4921 Exposition B'lvd.
Los Angeles, Calif.

Gordon's
1850 E. Pacific Coast Hy.
Long Beach, Calif.

J. J. Jewelcraft
2732 Colorado Blvd.
Los Angeles, Calif.

Jewelry Distributing Co.
315 West Fifth St.
Los Angeles, Calif.

Pacific Jewelers Supply
424 South Broadway
Los Angeles, Calif.

R & B Art-Craft Co.
11019 S. Vermont Ave.
Los Angeles, Calif.

Swartchild & Co.
448 S. Hill St.
Los Angeles, Calif.

Grieger's
1633 E. Walnut St.
Pasadena, Calif.

The Janmar Co.
507 Granger Bldg.
San Diego, Calif.

American Handicraft Co.
1110 Mission St.
San Francisco, Calif.

American Handicraft Co.
328 S. Colfax
Denver, Colo.

United Tool & Material
307 University Bldg.
Denver, Colorado

American Handicraft Co.
242 Spring St. N.W.
Atlanta, Ga.

Swartchild & Co.
23 Broad St. S.W.
Atlanta, Ga.

American Handicraft Co.
83 W. Van Buren
Chicago, Ill.

Bartlett & Co.
5 South Wabash Ave.
Chicago 3, Ill.

Swartchild & Co.
22 W. Madison St.
Chicago, Illinois

Alessi
16 East Central Blvd.
Villa Park, Ill.

Brennan Brothers
723 Odd Fellows Building
South Bend, Ind.

L. J. Pracht Jr. & Co.
251 N. Broadway
Wichita, Kansas

New Orleans Jewelers
206 Chartres St.
New Orleans, La.

Arts & Crafts Distributors
9520 Baltimore Ave.
College Park, Md.

Harry Parritz & Bro.
387 Washington St.
Boston, Mass.

C. W. Somers & Co.
387 Washington St.
Boston, Mass.

Swartchild & Co.
387 Washington St.
Boston, Mass.

American Handicraft Co.
4831 Woodword Ave.
Detroit, Mich.

C. R. Hill Co.
35 W. Grand River
Detroit, Mich.

Julius Garon Co.
317 W. Superior St.
Duluth, Minn.

C. R. Leeds Co.
627 1st Ave. No.
Minneapolis, Minnesota

Gager's Handicraft
1024 Nicollet Ave.
Minn. 2, Minn.

Swartchild & Co.
1207 Grand Ave.
Kansas City, Mo.

American Handicraft Co.
1710 Olive St.
St. Louis, Mo.

The Bergman Company
409 So. 15th St.
Omaha, Nebr.

William Dixon
32 East Kenney Street
Newark, New Jersey

R & R
50-A Van Houten St.
Paterson, N.J.

T. B. Hagstoz & Son
709 Sansome Street
Philadelphia, Pa.

Niagara Jewelry Supply
706 Brisbane Building
Buffalo, N.Y.

Allcraft
15 W. 45th St.
New York 36, N.Y.

Anchor Tool
12 John St.
New York City

American Handicraft Co.
33 E. 14th Street
New York City

Gamzon Bros.
15 West 47th St.
New York 36, N.Y.

Paul Gesswein
35 Maiden Lane
New York City

I. Shor
64 West 48th Street
New York City

Swartchild & Co.
331 Fourth Ave.
New York City, N.Y.

Akron Jewelers' Supply
1922 First Nat'l Bldg.
Akron, Ohio

The E. & J. Swigart Co.
34 W. Sixth Street
Cincinnati, Ohio

Ohio Jewelers Supply
1000 Schofield Building
Cleveland, Ohio

Columbus Jewelers Supply
82 N. High St.
Columbus, Ohio

Wm. Werkhaven & Son
2630 North High Street
Columbus, Ohio

Montana Assay Office
610 S.W. Second Ave.
Portland, Oregon

Meiskeys, Inc.
301 W. King St.
Lancaster, Penna.

American Handicraft Co.
1204 Walnut
Philadelphia, Pa.

Jos. B. Bechtel & Co., Inc.
729 Sansom St.
Phila., Pa.

Goldberg & Co.
124 S. 8th Street
Phila., Pa.

Keystone Jewelers Supply Co.
715 Sansom St.
Phila., Pa.

Ray Gaber
102 Century Bldg.
Pittsburgh, Pa.

C. Mancini & Son
96 Fountain Street
Providence 3, R.I.

Wm. R. Katz Co.
Irwin Keasler Bldg.
Dallas, Texas

Southwest Smelting & Refin.
1710 Jackson Street
Dallas 21, Texas

Swartchild & Co.
305½ S. Akard St.
Dallas, Texas

American Handicraft Co.
P. O. Box 1643
Fort Worth, Texas

Prague-Kurtz Co., Inc.
711 Main Street
Houston, Texas

American Handicraft Co.
164 E. 2nd S.
Salt Lake City, Utah

Primrose Jewelers Supplies
3rd Floor Ness Bldg.
Salt Lake City, Utah

Herr & Kline
400-404 Portlock Bldg.
Norfolk, Virginia

L. A. Clark Co.
1504 3rd Ave.
Seattle, Wash.

Swartchild & Co.
1318 Second Ave.
Seattle, Wash.

E. A. Gunther Company,
Brantford-Vancouver,

GOLD & SILVER

Handy and Harman
850 3rd Ave.
New York City

Rodman and Yarus
21 West 47th Street
New York City

MacClanahan
3461 Second Ave.
Sacramento, Calif.

Goldsmith Brothers
111 North Wabash Ave.
Chicago, Illinois

Wildberg Brothers
742 Market Street
San Francisco, Calif.

Southwest Refining Co.
P.O. Box 2010
Dallas 21, Texas

SILVER

J. J. Jewelcraft
2732 Colorado Blvd.
Los Angeles 41, Calif.

Hagstoz & Son
709 Sansom St.
Philadelphia, Pa.

COPPER & BRASS

William Dixon
32 East Kenney Street
Newark, New Jersey

Metal Goods Corporation
615 Rosedale Ave.
St. Louis 12, Mo.

PLATING SUPPLIES

Paul H. Gesswein
35 Maiden Lane
New York City

Hoover & Strong
117 W. Tupper St.
Buffalo 1, N.Y.

I. Shor
64 West 48th Street
New York City

William Dixon
32 East Kinney Street
Newark, New Jersey

CASTING SUPPLIES

Jewelry Casting Equipment
20 West 47th St.
New York 36, N.Y.

I. Shor
64 West 48th Street
New York City

Kerr Dental Mfg. Co.
Detroit, Mich.

GOLD & SILVER CASTINGS

Karbra Company
62 West 47th St.
New York City

ENAMELS

Thomas C. Thompson
1539 Deerfield Road
Highland Park, Illinois

American Handicraft Co.
All stores

PEARLS—CULTURED

I. Rosen
36 West 47th St.
New York 36, N.Y.

STONES

Mueller's
1000 E. Camelback
Phoenix, Ariz.

Bitner's
Scottsdale, Ariz.

Casa de Plata
1159 W. Casa Grande Rd.
Tucson, Ariz.

Davis' Rocks & Gems
1228 S. Stanton Ave.
Anaheim, Calif.

Terry's Lapidary
3616 E. Gage St.
Bell, Calif.

Belmont Lapidary
103 Ralston Ave.
Belmont, Calif.

MEB Jewelry & Lapidary
1444 El Camino Real
Belmont, Calif.

Minerals Unlimited
1724 University Ave.
Berkeley, Calif.

Norris Lapidary
1023 Calif. Drive
Burlingame, Calif.

Pascoes
1414 W. Glenoaks
Glendale, Calif.

H. & C. Green
812 N. Prairie Ave.
Hawthorne, Calif.

O'Brien Lapidary Equipment
1116 N. Wilcox Ave.
Hollywood 38, Calif.

Atlas Gems
6104 Whittier Blvd.
Los. Angeles, Calif.

Grapes Lapidary
4033A Judah St.
San Francisco, Calif.

Rainbow Gem
546 W. Mission Dr.
San Gabriel, Calif.

Bowsers
528 N. Milpas St.
Santa Barbara, Calif.

Shipley's Mineral House
Bayfield, Colo.

Uranium Corner, Inc.
2153 Broadway
Denver, Colorado

Rock & Shell Shop
2036 S. W. 57th Ave.
Miami 44, Fla.

Zoch's Rocks
4 N. 251 Swift Rd.
Addison, Ill.

Tom Robert's Rock Shop
1005 S. Michigan Ave.
Chicago 5, Ill.

Weidinger
625 West 54th Place
Chicago 9, Ill.

Rogmor Lapidiary
106 Fourth St.
Wilmette, Ill.

Brad's Rock Shop
903 W. 9 Mile Rd.
Ferndale 20, Mich.

Lake Superior Gem
203 E. Superior St.
Duluth, Minn.

Wm. J. Bingham
2100 Arcade St.
St. Paul 17, Minn.

International Gem
15 Maiden Lane
New York City

Sam Kramer
29 West 8th St.
New York City

Ace Lapidary
160-11 Hillside Ave.
Jamaica, N.Y.

Flick's Lapidary
1803 Millfair Rd.
Erie, Penna.

Lapidabrade
2407 Darby Rd.
Havertown, Pa.

Ray Van's
Salt Lake City
Utah

Ken Stewart's Gem Shop
136 W. South Simple
Salt Lake City, Utah

Murphy's
210 Altgelt Ave.
San Antonio, Texas

Fulmer's Agate Shop
5212 Rainier Ave.
Seattle 8, Wash.

Rozema's Rockpile
776 East Leonard
Grand Rapids 5, Mich.

JEWELRY DESIGNERS

Designs Technique
62 W. 47th St.
New York City

TRADE ASSOCIATIONS

American National Retail
Jewelry Ass'n
551 5th Ave.
New York 17, N.Y.

The Jewelry Crafts Ass'n
20 W. 47th Street
New York 19, N.Y.

Gemological Institute
541 S. Alexandria Ave.
Los Angeles 5, Calif.

Sterling Silversmiths Guild
551 Fifth Ave.
New York 17, N.Y.

JEWELRY UNION

International Jewelry
Workers Union, Local 1
133 West 44th St.
New York 19, N.Y.

MAGAZINES

National Jeweler
216 W. Jackson Blvd.
Chicago 6, Illinois

Jewelers Circular Keystone
Chestnut and 56 Street
Philadelphia 39, Pa.

Mineral Notes and News
Palmdale, Calif.

The Lapidary Journal
Del Mar, Calif.

Jewelers Buyers Guide
1819 Broadway
New York City

Craft Horizons
44 West 53rd St.
New York 17, N.Y.

REFERENCES

Art Monograms & Lettering
J. M. Bergling

Metalcraft and Jewelry
Emil Kronquist

Gems and Gem Material
Kraus and Holden

Enameling
Kenneth Bates

Jewelry Making
K. Winebrenner

Artistic Metalwork
A. F. Bick

The Silversmith
Geoffrey Holden

Art Metal Work
Emil F. Kronquist

Metalwork and Enamelling
Herbert Maryon

INDEX